KEYSTONES for READING

COMPREHENSION ▪ VOCABULARY ▪ STUDY SKILLS

Level B

Alden J. Moe, Ph.D.
Louisiana State University

Sandra S. Dahl, Ph.D.
University of Wisconsin

Carol J. Hopkins, Ph.D.
Purdue University

John W. Miller, Ph.D.
Georgia Southern College

Elayne Ackerman Moe, M.Ed.
Louisiana State Department of Education

MODERN CURRICULUM PRESS
Cleveland ● Toronto

Table of Contents

Words That Make Your Mouth Water

Food is important in our lives. Some food makes us grow strong and healthy. Some is just plain fun to eat. In this lesson, you will use your ideas about food. You will learn to sort out your ideas.

---

 1 KEYS to Grouping

Words have families, too.

LEARN An orange is related to an apple. They are both in the fruit family.

DIRECTIONS Read the list of words. You will find the name of a word family, or group, and the names of three group members. Circle the word that names the whole group.

carrots   spinach   vegetables   lettuce

 2 Practice Grouping

DIRECTIONS Words can be grouped in different ways. Look at the words you did not circle. Sort them into new groups. Write them on the lines.

Foods I Like   Foods I Don't Like

_____   _____

_____   _____

_____   _____

DIRECTIONS Circle the words that name food. Put them in the right group.

My father says I should drink water. I do, but I like soft drinks, too. My mother says I should eat carrots and celery. I do, but I like potato chips, too. My parents say I should eat apples and cheese for snacks. I do, but I like ice cream, too.

Sometimes I tell my mother I want her to serve candy and cake for dinner. I really know better, though. I'm lucky she doesn't. I want to grow up strong and healthy.

Foods to Have More Of

_____

_____

_____

_____

Foods to Have Less Of

_____

_____

_____

_____

REMEMBER Words can be sorted into groups.

New Puppies

Making choices can be hard. In this lesson, you will read about a family who had to choose names for new puppies. You will learn how words that describe helped them make their choices.

 ## KEYS to Adjectives

Adjectives tell more.

LEARN Adjectives are words that help you see pictures more clearly when you read. The sentences below show how adjectives make reading more interesting.

EXAMPLE Without adjectives: The puppy wagged its tail.
With adjectives: The **tiny gray** puppy wagged its **stubby** tail.

DIRECTIONS Read the incomplete sentences. Think of a word that can tell more about the word in dark print. Write it on the line. The word you write will be an adjective.

1. Sally lost one of her _____ **mittens.**

2. A skyscraper is a _____ **building.**

3. Richie has two _____ **sisters.**

Practice With Adjectives

DIRECTIONS Read the story about building a doghouse. Then use the adjectives in dark print to complete the drawing.

When summer vacation started, Mike and Jennifer needed something to do. They decided to build a **pretty** doghouse for Heidi.

First they found some **old** boards. They pounded them together. Beside the door, they cut a **square** window. Just for fun, they used a **cardboard** box to make a **tall** chimney.

Then they were ready to paint. Mike painted the doghouse **yellow,** while Jenny painted the roof **blue.** They made the chimney red. They drew **fake** bricks on the chimney with **black** paint.

They weren't finished yet. They hung **green** curtains in the window, and planted **small purple** pansies under it. Finally, they did the most important job of all. They painted the word Heidi over the door in **big black** letters.

Jenny and Mike looked at the new house. They were proud. Heidi was happy. The new doghouse would keep her cool on the hot summer days.

Read and Apply

DIRECTIONS Read the story. Watch for adjectives.

Polly ran into her classroom. She had a sign in her hand. The sign said, ''Puppies for sale! To good homes only.''

''Miss Penn,'' she cried. ''May I put this sign on the bulletin board? It's time to find homes for our new puppies.''

The other children crowded around Polly. They wanted to know all about the puppies.

''Everyone sit down,'' said Miss Penn. ''Polly will tell the whole class about her puppies.''

''Six weeks ago,'' said Polly, ''our dog Buttons had puppies. She had a litter of four. Now they are almost old enough to have new homes.

''When the puppies were born, they were very tiny. Their eyes were closed. Their fur was short and shiny. They looked like little rats. They weren't much fun. All they wanted to do was sleep. They stayed close to Buttons, and she took good care of them.

''After a while, though, they started to get really cute. Their eyes opened. They ran and played with each other. They wanted to explore.

''Daddy said we should give the puppies names. That was hard. No one could agree on what to call them.

''One night we had a family meeting to decide on names. Mom said to look at the puppies and think about words to describe how they looked or how they acted. Then it was easier to name them.

''One puppy is all black. It was easy to name that puppy. We named him Blackie. Blackie's sister looks just like him, except for one thing. She has a big spot over one eye. We decided to call her Spot.

''The third puppy is black and white. He looks a little different

from Blackie and Spot. He has a long tail that curls up over his back. His name is Curly.

"The fourth puppy is the smallest of all. She is the one that gets into the most trouble. She was the first to climb out of the box. She barks the most. She runs and jumps the most. She has the most energy. My mom said a good adjective for her would be frisky."

"I'll bet you called that one Frisky!" shouted Tommy.

The children enjoyed Polly's story. Some already had pets of their own. Some children lived in places where dogs weren't allowed. Four of the children went home to ask their parents if they could have a puppy. By the next day, all four puppies had good homes.

DIRECTIONS Look at the pictures of the four puppies. Look back in the story to find the adjectives that describe each one. Write each puppy's name on the line below it.

_____

_____

_____

_____

REMEMBER Adjectives describe other words.

Grandpa's Gift

How would you decide between two gifts if they both looked the same? In this lesson, you will read about a boy who had to make that choice. You will also learn about words that mean almost the same thing.

 KEYS to Synonyms

Synonyms help you say the same thing in different ways.

LEARN Use both words in the same sentence. If the sentence has the same meaning both times, the two words are synonyms.

EXAMPLE Grandpa brought me a gift.
Grandpa brought me a present.

DIRECTIONS Read each sentence. The underlined word has a synonym. Find its synonym in the box. Write it on the line.

close	woods	receive	hair

1. I like to get presents. _____

2. Some animals have fur. _____

3. Please shut the cage door. _____

4. Many animals live in the forest. _____

Read the words on each pair of presents. If the two words are synonyms, color the presents the same color. If they are not synonyms, color each gift a different color.

house

home

gnaw

chew

small

large

open

shut

kind

nice

big

hug

decide

choose

right

correct

kid

child

Read the story. Watch for synonyms.

When Grandpa came to visit, he brought Chris two gifts. One had a blue bow. The other had a red bow. One box seemed broken. It had holes in the top.

Chris looked at the presents. He didn't know which to open first. He pointed from one box to the other and chanted: "Eenie, meenie, minie, moe. Which one first I do not know. Red, blue, red, blue, red, blue bow. Eenie, meenie, minie, moe."

Chris chose the gift with the blue bow. He untied the ribbon and peeled off the paper. When he opened the box, he found a bag filled with wood shavings. He also saw what looked like a bag of seeds.

Chris wondered why Grandpa had given him such a strange gift. He looked at Grandpa. Grandpa was grinning.

"Open the other gift," he said.

Chris opened the box with the red bow and the holes. Something was moving inside. Suddenly Chris laughed. He reached into the box and picked up a furry ball in each hand.

"Look, Grandpa. Now I know what the other presents are for. They are food and bedding for my hamsters. I'll name them Fuzzy and Fluffy, but which one is which?"

Chris pointed from one hamster to the other. He sang: "Eenie, meenie, minie, moe. Hamsters run fast, to and fro. Now they stop and now they go. Eenie, meenie, minie, moe."

"This is Fuzzy, and this is Fluffy," said Chris. "Both names mean almost the same thing. If I say the wrong name, it won't be too bad a mistake. Thank you, Grandpa. This is the best present ever."

Find a phrase in the story that means almost the same thing as each group of words below. Find the synonym for the underlined word. Write it on the line.

1. had <u>arrived</u> with two gifts _____

2. which to <u>unwrap</u> first _____

3. <u>picked</u> the gift with the blue bow _____

4. peeled off the <u>wrapping</u> _____

5. <u>spied</u> what looked a bag of seeds _____

6. such an <u>odd</u> gift _____

7. He was <u>smiling</u>. _____

8. opened the <u>container</u> with the red bow _____

9. <u>See</u>, Grandpa. Now I know _____

10. I'll <u>call</u> them Fuzzy and Fluffy _____

11. She <u>chanted</u>: _____

12. Now they <u>halt</u> and now they go. _____

13. say the <u>incorrect</u> name _____

14. won't be too <u>awful</u> a mistake _____

15. the <u>finest</u> present ever _____

REMEMBER Synonyms mean almost the same thing.

Patrick Says Goodbye

Would you rather feel happy or sad? In this lesson, you will read about a boy who feels sad when his best friend moves away. When he makes new friends, he feels just the opposite of sad. You will learn words which have opposite meanings.

 ## KEYS to Antonyms

Antonyms are words with opposite meanings.

EXAMPLE   Jesse went up the stairs.   Gerry ran home.
          Jesse went down the stairs.   Gerry walked home.

DIRECTIONS   Read each word in the column on the left. Write the letter of its antonym.

_____ 1. big	**a.** back	
_____ 2. top	**b.** outside	
_____ 3. off	**c.** under	
_____ 4. go	**d.** little	
_____ 5. buy	**e.** bottom	
_____ 6. inside	**f.** stop	
_____ 7. front	**g.** on	
_____ 8. over	**h.** sell	

2 Practice With Antonyms

DIRECTIONS Read each pair of words. Circle the pairs that are antonyms. Write each antonym pair on opposite ends of a seesaw.

1. begin   end
2. heads   tails
3. hard   easy
4. line   lone

5. first   last
6. write   tight
7. dark   light
8. above below

9. wrong   right
10. raw   cooked
11. large   huge
12. lick   stick

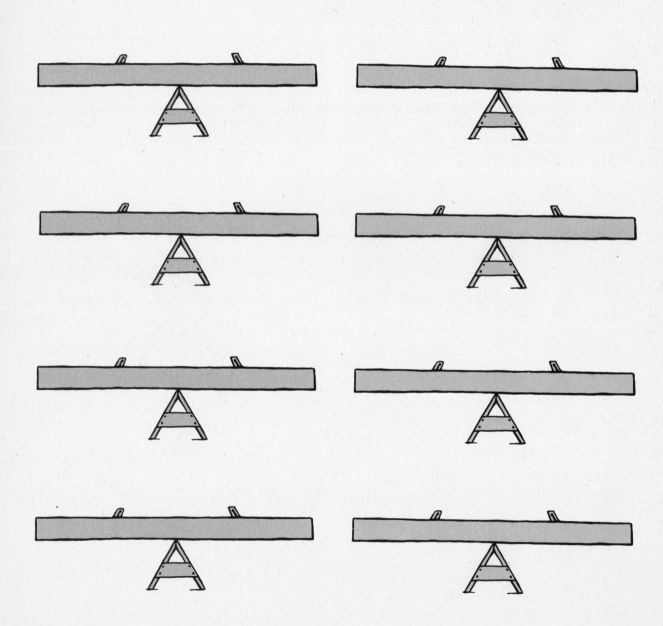

DIRECTIONS Read the story. Watch for antonyms.

Patrick and Ben were buddies. They did everything together. They thought they would be going to school together, too. But Ben moved.

On moving day, Patrick watched from his front yard. Ben came over to where Patrick stood.

"We are leaving now," said Ben. Patrick did not say anything. "Well, I have to go now," said Ben. "Good-bye."

"GOOD-BYE!" shouted Patrick. He turned and ran into his house. He banged the door closed. Ben and his family drove down the street and out of sight.

Patrick felt funny when school began. There were many boys and girls he did not know. He sat at a desk in the corner. He hoped no one would be able to see him there.

"Would you like to use the watercolors?" asked the teacher.

Patrick folded his arms. "No, thanks. Who wants to paint without Ben!" he grumbled.

At recess Patrick stood at the edge of the playground. A boy from his class ran up to him. "Want to play ball?" he asked.

Patrick turned and walked away. "Dumb old Ben anyway," he mumbled.

At lunch Patrick found an empty bench. He opened his lunchbox. A girl with red curls sat down across from him. She looked at Patrick as if she were inspecting a bug.

"What are you looking at?" Patrick growled.

"Why don't you like anyone?" asked the girl.

"What do you mean?" asked Patrick.

"You act like you don't want any friends," said the girl.

"I have a friend," said Patrick. "Ben."

"Who is Ben?" asked the girl.

"My friend," said Patrick. "Only he moved."

"Is there a rule that says you can have only one friend?" the red-headed girl asked.

Patrick thought. "I guess not."

"Will you play ball with us?" she asked.

Patrick thought again. Then he nodded his head. "OK."

Patrick made many friends at lunch. He had fun! When he got home, there was something waiting for him.

"Ben wrote you a letter," said Patrick's mother. Patrick read the letter out loud to Mother. He smiled. He felt good.

Patrick and Ben are still buddies. Now they write and tell each other everything they do.

DIRECTIONS Change a word in each sentence to make the sentence true. Choose an antonym from the box for each underlined word. Write the antonym on the line.

stay	good	sat	smiled	good-bye
happy	everything	leaving	friends	empty

1. Patrick was <u>sad</u> to get a letter from Ben. _____

2. Patrick felt <u>bad</u> when he read Ben's letter. _____

3. "<u>Hello!</u>" shouted Patrick as Ben left. _____

4. Patrick did <u>nothing</u> with Ben. _____

5. Ben's family was <u>arriving</u>. _____

6. Patrick <u>stood</u> at a desk in the corner. _____

7. Patrick <u>frowned</u> as he read Ben's letter. _____

8. Patrick wanted Ben to <u>go</u>. _____

9. Patrick found a(n) <u>full</u> bench at lunch. _____

10. Ben and Patrick were <u>enemies</u>. _____

REMEMBER Antonyms have opposite meanings.

14 Antonyms

A Perfect Day

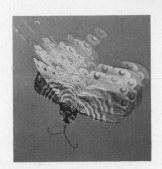

Can you hear the neigh of a hoarse horse?
Are two cookies too many?

Two words in each question sound alike, but
are spelled differently. Do they mean the same
thing? In this lesson, you will learn about more
pairs of words like these.

 ## KEYS to Homonyms

**Homonyms sound alike, but have different
spellings and meanings.**

EXAMPLE hoarse-rough and raspy   Greg had a hoarse voice.
horse-a large animal   Jenny likes to ride her horse.

DIRECTIONS Read each pair of homonyms and their meanings. Then
read each sentence to see which meaning makes sense. Write the letter of
the word that belongs in the sentence.

a. hole-a part cut out   **c.** heal-to make well

b. whole-complete   **d.** heel-a part of the foot

1. I ate the _____ thing.

2. There is a _____ in my sock.

3. I have a blister on my _____

4. This will help it to _____

2 Practice With Homonyms

DIRECTIONS Read each sentence. Choose the word that will correctly complete the sentence. Write it on the line.

1. The baby bird was too _____ to fly.

2. Dad will be out of town next

   _____ .

week   weak

3. The wind made the boat _____ through the water.

4. I bought this on _____ .

sail   sale

5. The _____ was rough all day.

6. I _____ you are feeling better.

see   sea

7. We went shopping for new _____ .

8. Please _____ your eyes and wait.

close   clothes

16 Homonyms

3 Read and Apply

DIRECTIONS Read the story. Watch for homonyms.

Juan looked outside. The sky was blue with some pale clouds. The sun was shining. A strong wind blew. It was the perfect day.

Juan dialed the phone. He hoped Gil was home. He just had to be. Juan heard ring after ring. Where was Gil? He would miss the whole thing.

Juan hung up and looked outside. He couldn't stand to wait another day. Besides, they'd agreed he should go if the weather was right. He'd just have to go alone.

He ran up the stairs. There lay the kite he and Gil had worked so hard to make. Too bad Gil wasn't here to fly it for the first time. They had convinced Mom to buy all those balls of string at the garage sale. Then they had worked on the kite every day. Just last night they had made the tail.

Juan grabbed a jacket from the clothes tree and ran out of the room. He was off to fly the new kite! Just then he heard three short raps on the door. It was Gil. That was their code. Juan flew down the stairs to the door. There stood Gil, out of breath.

"I ran all the way," puffed Gil. "I hoped you would still be here. I told Dad we had to hurry. I knew today would be perfect!"

The boys raced along the path beside the road to the open field. They worked together to get the kite off the ground. Together they held the string as the kite swayed upward.

"It works," yelled Juan. "It really works!"

"Of course it works," answered Gil. "We finished just in time for this perfect kite-flying day."

DIRECTIONS The story you just read has many words that have homonyms. Read each word below. Find its underlined homonym in the story. Write the word from the story on the line.

1. rode _____
2. knew _____
3. sew _____
4. blew _____
5. sail _____
6. maid _____
7. by _____
8. four _____
9. tale _____
10. hole _____
11. wood _____
12. stares _____
13. wee _____
14. coarse _____

15. son _____
16. close _____
17. hear _____
18. wraps _____
19. pail _____
20. two _____
21. flu _____
22. sum _____
23. herd _____
24. bee _____
25. write _____
26. there _____
27. weigh _____
28. buoys _____

REMEMBER Homonyms only sound alike.

All About Earthworms

When you read, you are a detective. You find clues to understand the words. In this lesson, you will figure out words by putting clues together. You will learn about earthworms.

 ## KEYS to Context Clues

Look at the words before and after the word you want to learn. Those words are the context.

LEARN Suppose you need to know the word <u>submerged</u>. Read the sentence: Earthworms can live <u>submerged</u> in water. You know from the sentence that <u>submerged</u> has something to do with water.

You know you can swim in water, float on water, or go under water. Does the word <u>submerged</u> remind you of any other word you know? How about <u>submarine</u>? A submarine can go under water.

If you guessed from the context clues that <u>submerged</u> means "under water," you were correct.

DIRECTIONS Read each sentence. Use context clues to figure out the meaning of the underlined word. Answer the questions.

When the weather is very dry, earthworms dig deep into the ground. There they find the <u>moisture</u> they need.

a. Write a clue from the sentence. _____

b. Write a clue from your head. _____

c. <u>Moisture</u> means   1. dryness 2. dampness 3. heat

DIRECTIONS Read the paragraphs. Use context clues to figure out the meaning of the underlined words. Put a check on the line in front of the correct meaning.

1. Earthworms come in many varieties. Some kinds are very tiny. One kind of earthworm that lives in Australia may grow up to be twelve feet (about 3.6 meters) long.

   _____ **a.** colors

   _____ **b.** kinds

   _____ **c.** changes

2. It is easy to see the rings that make up an earthworm's body. They are clearly visible to the naked eye.

   _____ **a.** easily seen

   _____ **b.** able to be heard

   _____ **c.** very round

3. There are many different kinds of earthworms. The rings on an earthworm's body make it easy to distinguish between the different kinds.

   _____ **a.** put out

   _____ **b.** tell apart

   _____ **c.** to ignore

4. In summer, when the weather is hot, the earthworm digs itself deep into the ground, where it is cool and damp. In winter, it burrows far down into the warmer earth.

   _____ **a.** falls

   _____ **b.** rises

   _____ **c.** digs a tunnel

5. Earthworms have little bristles on their rings. The bristles make it easier for the worms to move. They help the worms hang on to the sides of their burrows.

   _____ **a.** stiff, prickly hairs

   _____ **b.** fragile sticks

   _____ **c.** energies

Read and Apply

DIRECTIONS Read the poem about worms. If you find any words you don't know, use context to figure them out.

Worms and the Wind

Worms would rather be
    worms.
Ask a worm and he says,
    "Who knows what a worm
    knows?"
Worms go down and up and
    over and under.
Worms like tunnels.
When worms talk they talk
    about the worm world.
Worms like it in the dark.
Neither the sun nor the moon
    interests a worm.
Zigzag worms hate circle
    worms.
Curve worms never trust
    square worms.
Worms know what worms
    want.
Slide worms are suspicious of
    crawl worms.
One worm asks another, "How
    does your belly drag
    today?"
The shape of a crooked worm
satisfies a crooked worm.
A straight worm says, "Why
    not be straight?"
Worms tired of crawling begin
    to slither.
Long worms slither farther than
    short worms.
Middle-sized worms say, "It is
    nice to be neither long nor
    short."
Old worms teach young worms
    to say, "Don't be sorry for
    me unless you have lived
    in worm places and read
    worm books."
When worms go to war they
    dig in, come out and fight,
    dig in again, and so on.
Worms underground never hear
    the wind overground and
    sometimes they ask,
    "What is this wind we
    hear of?"

—Carl Sandburg

Find each underlined word in the poem you just read. Write the letter of its correct meaning on the line. Use what you know and use context clues.

1. A <u>tunnel</u> is _____.

    a. an underground passage

    b. an open pit

    c. a bridge over water

2. A <u>suspicious</u> worm would _____.

    a. like to be a crawl worm

    b. think other worms were guilty

    c. trust most other worms

3. A worm whose belly <u>drags</u> would _____.

    a. be a different shape

    b. move along the ground slowly

    c. hold its belly high

4. A <u>crooked</u> worm would be _____.

    a. bent, twisted, or curved

    b. very smooth and straight

    c. flat from end to end

5. <u>Satisfies</u> means almost the same as _____.

    a. dislikes

    b. pleases

    c. changes

6. A worm that <u>slithers</u> _____.

    a. stays completely still

    b. rolls and turns

    c. slides or glides

REMEMBER Use context with clues in your head to figure out new words.

Monica's Funny Fish

How does an elephant get ready for a trip?
He packs his trunk, of course.

   That joke is funny because the word <u>trunk</u> has more than one meaning. In this lesson, you will learn more words with more than one meaning. You will read about a strange fish.

 ## KEYS to Choosing the Correct Meaning

Read the whole sentence carefully.

LEARN   Read the two meanings for the word <u>saw</u>: 1) looked at, 2) a cutting tool. Which meaning is correct for each sentence below?

1. This sharp saw will cut wood quickly.
2. When they looked toward the lake, they saw many boats.

   The correct meaning depends on the rest of the sentence. In the first sentence, <u>sharp</u>, <u>cut</u>, and <u>wood</u> tell you meaning number 2 is correct. In the second sentence, <u>looked</u> tells you to choose meaning number 1.

DIRECTIONS Read the meanings and the sentences below. Write the number of the correct meaning on the line before each sentence.

1) the outside covering of a tree   2) a sound made by a dog

_____ **1.** The puppy's bark woke us.

_____ **2.** The bark on the branches and trunk is dark brown.

Practice Using Words With Many Meanings

DIRECTIONS You have read about words with more than one meaning. ZANG is a word with no meaning. ZANG is not a real word.

Cross out ZANG in each sentence below. Choose the correct word from the box, and write it above the word you crossed out.

bend	light	run	fly	ring

1. We heard the recess bell ZANG.

   She wore a tiny ZANG on her finger.

2. The school is near a ZANG in the road.

   Can the strong man ZANG this steel pipe?

3. Airplanes ZANG through the clouds.

   I swatted the ZANG buzzing around my head.

4. The sun gives ZANG to plants.

   The bag of sand was not ZANG

5. I can ZANG around the track seven times.

   Kevin scored the winning ZANG in the baseball game.

Read and Apply

Read all about the strange fish Monica caught. The words in boldface type can have more than one meaning.

Early one morning, Dad came to wake Monica up.

"Wake up!" he said. "It's a perfect day for the first fishing **trip** of the season. May I borrow some change from your piggy **bank?** I need to buy a new fishing license."

"Sure," said Monica. "Then we can **head** straight for the river."

Dad packed the **trunk** with the things they would need. Then they were ready to go.

"**Wave** to Mom," Dad said, as they pulled down the driveway.

Monica watched for a **sign** that said "Fishing Licenses."

"There it is," she said. "I can tell by the long **line** of people in front."

Finally, it was their turn at the window. Dad had to **sign** his name on the line.

When they got to the river, they sat on the grassy **bank.** Monica dropped her **feet** over the edge. Then she cast her fishing **line.** It made a little **wave** in the water. Monica and Dad leaned back against a tree **trunk** and waited. Soon she felt a tug.

Monica stood up. She could see a huge fish just under the water. She was so excited, she was afraid she would **trip.**

"I caught one, Dad," she shouted. "It's two **feet** long and it has whiskers. It looks like a monster."

Dad shook his **head.**

"It isn't a monster," he said. "It doesn't have whiskers. Those things that look like whiskers are called barbels. That fish uses them to find food. They do look like a cat's whiskers, though. That's why people call those strange fish catfish."

A. sign   1. 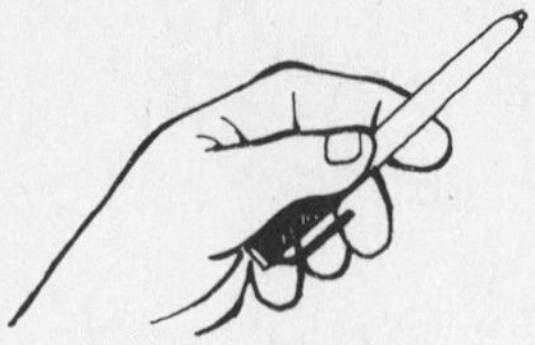   2. 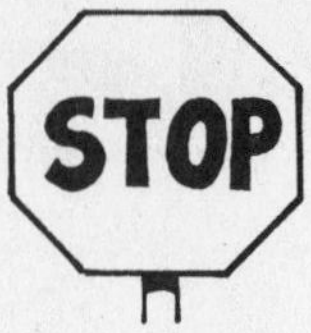   STOP

1. _____

2. _____

B. wave 1. 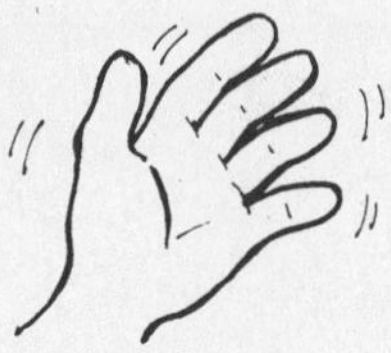   2.

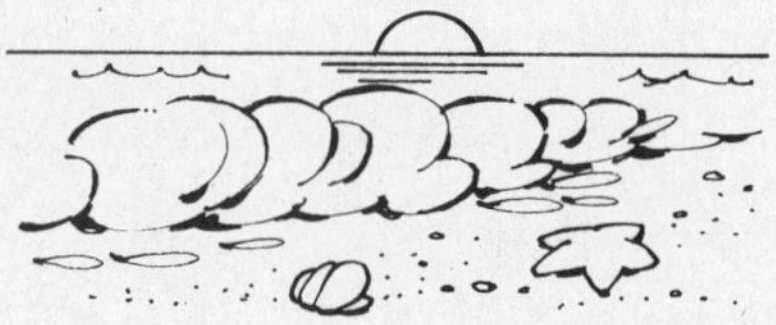

1. _____

2. _____

C. line 1. 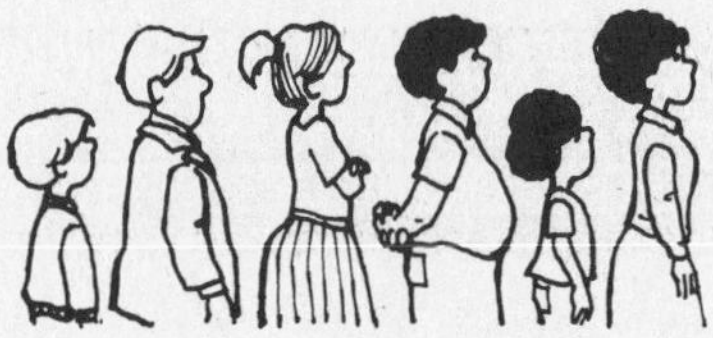   2.

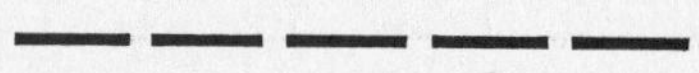

1. _____

2. _____

D. bank 1. 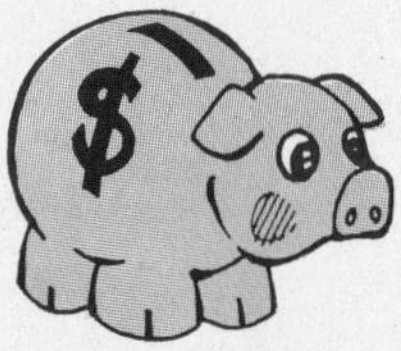   2.

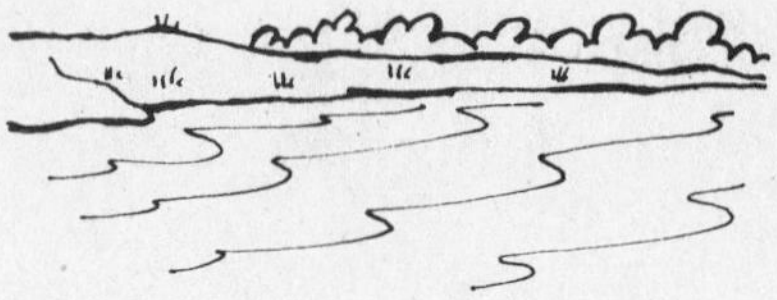

1. _____

2. _____

E. feet 1. 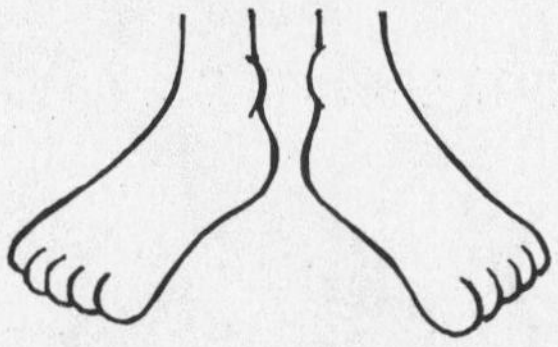   2.

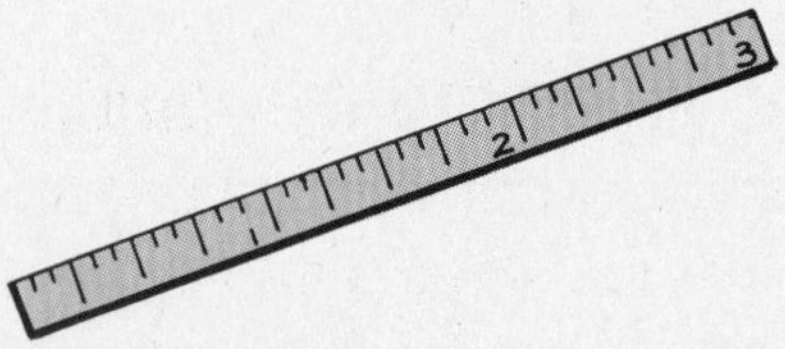

1. _____

2. _____

REMEMBER One word can have more than one meaning.

The Party

Parties are fun. In this lesson, you will read about a party where the guests gave gifts in an unusual way. You will learn to combine words like the guests combined gifts.

 ## KEYS to Contractions

Contractions are shortcut words.

LEARN Some words can be combined to make one shorter word. That shorter word is called a contraction. When you make a contraction, you leave some letters out of one of the words. An apostrophe takes the place of the letters you left out. This is an apostrophe: '.

EXAMPLE you + will = you'll   they + are = they're

DIRECTIONS Read the invitation. Write the contractions on the line.

Date: Saturday, May 4
Time: 4:00 P.M.
Place: 224 Main Street
For: Debbie Johnson

You're invited to my party. I've made special plans. We'll have lots of fun. I can't wait to see you. Please don't miss it.

1. _____ 2. _____ 3. _____ 4. _____ 5. _____

Contractions **27**

2 Practice With Contractions

DIRECTIONS Read the pairs of words on the birthday cake. Each pair can be combined to make a contraction. Find a word pair on the cake that matches each contraction in a balloon. Write its number on the line in the balloon.

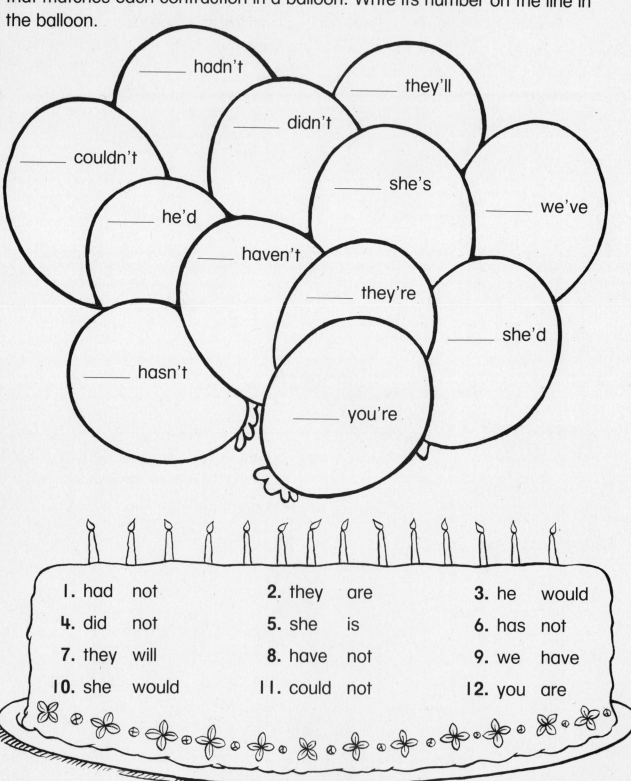

_____ hadn't

_____ they'll

_____ didn't

_____ couldn't

_____ she's

_____ we've

_____ he'd

_____ haven't

_____ they're

_____ she'd

_____ hasn't

_____ you're

1. had   not   2. they   are   3. he   would
4. did   not   5. she   is   6. has   not
7. they   will   8. have   not   9. we   have
10. she   would   11. could   not   12. you   are

3 Read and Apply

DIRECTIONS Read the story. See how things go together.

Everyone was excited about the party. Everyone wanted to make it a special birthday, but no one knew just how.

Finally Amy had an idea. Two people could get together. They'd get one gift with two parts, like a pair of mittens. Debbie could have fun matching up the gifts.

"That's a good idea!" said Joel. "Let's be sure to keep the secret."

The kids couldn't wait for her to open the gifts. They giggled as she unwrapped the first one. Debbie was surprised to find one striped kneesock. Everyone laughed louder.

Then Debbie opened a book. It was called Adventures in Space, Part 2. She wondered if she should read Part 1 first. "There's something funny going on," she thought. Debbie opened the third gift and found the matching knee sock.

Then Debbie laughed louder than anyone.

"It's a good joke," she said. "You sure fooled me."

After that, Debbie had fun opening her gifts and combining them to make a whole present. When she'd opened the last gift, she had one thing left over.

"This is strange," Debbie said. "All my other gifts were in pairs. This pretty blue bowl doesn't seem to go with anything."

Just then Mom walked in. She was carrying a little white ball of fur. It had a blue bow around its neck.

"I'd like to join the fun, too," she said. "What do you think? Isn't this little kitten a good match for that blue food bowl?"

Debbie cuddled the kitten. What a great birthday!

This time, take one word and change it into two. Read the contraction before each sentence. Read the sentence. Then write the two words it was made from on the line. Read the sentence once more. Does it still make sense?

1. (They'd) _____ _____ get one gift with two parts.

2. (That's) _____ _____ a good idea.

3. (Let's) _____ _____ be sure to keep the secret.

4. (couldn't) The kids _____ _____ wait.

5. (There's) _____ _____ something funny going on.

6. (It's) _____ _____ a good joke.

7. (She'd) _____ _____ opened the last gift.

8. (doesn't) This pretty blue bowl _____ _____ go with anything.

9. (I'd) _____ _____ like to join the fun, too.

10. (Isn't) _____ _____ this little kitten a good match for the blue bowl?

REMEMBER Put an apostrophe in when you take letters out.

Tommy Makes Breakfast

To make a good meal, you put together your favorite foods. To make a compound word, you put words together instead. In this lesson you will read about a boy who can put together a good meal. You will learn to put words together to make compound words.

KEYS to Compound Words

One Word + One Word = One Word

LEARN A long word can look hard. One kind of long word is easier than it looks. That is a compound word. Compound words are easy to read when you know how to take them apart. A compound word is a word that is made by putting two smaller words together.

EXAMPLE inside = in + side   something = some + thing

DIRECTIONS Break each compound word into its two smaller parts. Each part must be a whole word by itself.

1. toothpaste = _____ + _____
2. fingernail = _____ + _____
3. cupcake   = _____ + _____
4. everything = _____ + _____
5. doorknob   = _____ + _____

DIRECTIONS Read each sentence. Find the compound word and circle it. Then write the two parts of each compound word on the lines.

1. Bonnie left her notebook on the table.

   _____ _____

2. Rover slept soundly in the doghouse.

   _____ _____

3. Get some wood for the fireplace.

   _____ _____

4. The moonlight helped us find our way.

   _____ _____

5. Juanita put strawberry jam on her toast.

   _____ _____

6. Gloria made footprints in the fresh snow.

   _____ _____

7. The basketball star was six feet tall.

   _____ _____

8. A small brown bird flew out of the birdhouse.

   _____ _____

9. The airplane holds over one hundred passengers.

   _____ _____

10. Our favorite picnic spot is near the waterfall.

    _____ _____

11. Harold got a sunburn when he stayed out too long.

    _____ _____

12. The school newspaper had a story about our class field trip.

    _____ _____

Read and Apply

DIRECTIONS Read the story about the surprise Tommy cooked up for his parents. Use the words in the box to make compound words. Write them on the lines to complete the story.

thing	berry	blue	corn	pan	oat	over
thing	cakes	cross	news	bread	some	out
side	paper	made	over	word	home	meal
break	bed	berry	made	fast	weight	room
home	every	weight	straw			

One Saturday morning Tommy decided to do _____nice for his parents. He would make _____ . He would take them breakfast in bed.

First he made _____ . Next he made _____ . Then he warmed up some _____and buttered it. He put _____jam on the tray. Finally, he ran _____to get the morning _____ . He knew his father would want to do the _____puzzle. When _____was ready, he took the tray to he door of his parents'

_____ .

"Surprise, Mom! Surprise, Dad! I've brought you a _____ breakfast," said Tommy.

"Wow!" said Dad. "If I eat like this every day, I'll be _____in no time."

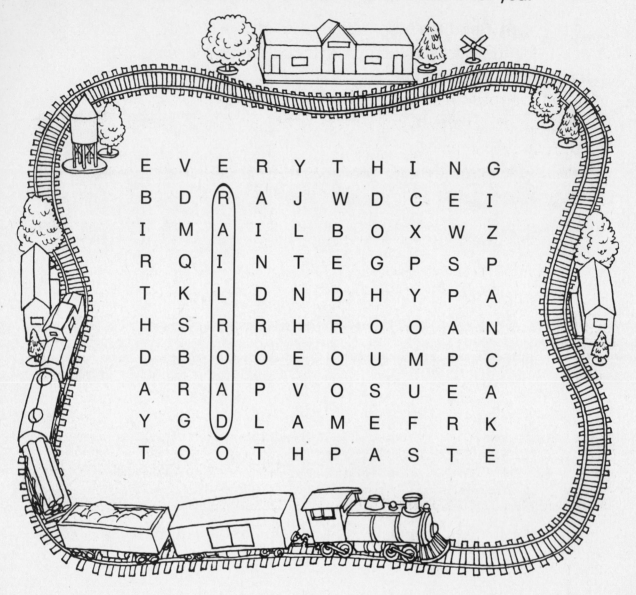

```
E V E R Y T H I N G
B D R A J W D C E I
I M A I L B O X W Z
R Q I N T E G P S P
T K L D D H Y P A N
H S R R H R O O A N
D B O O E O U M P C
A R A P V O S U E A
Y G D L A M E F R K
T O O T H P A S T E
```

1. railroad _____   6. _____

2. _____   7. _____

3. _____   8. _____

4. _____   9. _____

5. _____   10. _____

REMEMBER Take a compound apart, and you'll have two words.

Grasshoppers

I am an insect. I live in the grass. I am a hopper. You can guess my name by putting together the word for where I live with the word that tells how I move. What am I?

In this lesson, you will read about the insect whose name is made from two words. You will learn more about compound words.

KEYS to Compound Words

A compound word is one word made from two.

EXAMPLE   row + boat = rowboat

DIRECTIONS Put two words together to make a compound word. Print the new word on the line.

1. sail + boat = _____

2. hair + cut = _____

3. cook + book = _____

4. base + ball = _____

5. side + walk = _____

6. pan + cake = _____

7. birth + day = _____

8. meat + ball = _____

9. door + way = _____

10. work + shop = _____

11. sun + light = _____

12. space + suit = _____

13. snow + man = _____

14. air + plane = _____

15. up + stairs = _____

16. rain + coat = _____

DIRECTIONS Use the compound words you made to complete these sentences. Write the correct compound on each line.

1. Mark will be nine on his next _____.

2. Jane is playing _____ in the yard.

3. I ate a big _____ for breakfast.

4. Mike went to the barber for a _____.

5. Kelly climbed _____ to the attic.

6. I wear a _____ on rainy days.

7. We rode in a _____ on the lake.

8. The _____ melted in the sun.

9. We played hopscotch on the _____.

10. Dad found a new recipe in the _____.

11. The _____ landed on the runway.

12. I have a _____ sandwich
    in my lunchbox.

13. The astronaut wore a _____.

14. Plants make food from _____.

15. Mom found the saw in the _____.

16. The sofa will not fit through the _____.

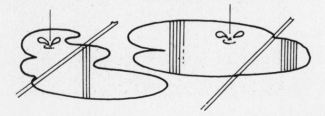

DIRECTIONS Read the story. Watch for compound words.

Grasshoppers have a hard covering on the outside of their bodies. They do not have bones inside their bodies, like people. The body of a grasshopper is divided into three parts: the head, the thorax, and the abdomen. The grasshopper has ears, but they are in a strange place. The ears are on the grasshopper's sides. Grasshoppers use their front legs to keep themselves clean. The mother grasshopper digs holes and lays eggs underground.

There are two main kinds of grasshoppers. Shorthorn grasshoppers are the kind we see most often. They eat farmland crops and spit if you try to catch them. Longhorn grasshoppers have long feelers and like to move at nighttime.

These six-legged jumping insects can be found in almost any backyard or empty lot in the summertime. If you look quickly, you may see a green grasshopper jump out of the grass. You may have trouble seeing it after it lands. Its green coloring helps it hide so it can get food and keep from becoming food for other animals.

When a grasshopper grows too big for its baby skin, the skin dries and splits, and the grasshopper climbs out of it. At first, the new skin is soft, but it soon becomes hard like one of your fingernails. Grasshoppers may change skins many times during their lives.

The next time you are outside on a warm summer day, be sure to look for the wonderful six-legged jumping animal with ears on its sides.

Underline the compound word in each sentence. Write its two parts on the lines beside the sentence.

1. Grasshoppers are strange insects. _____ _____

2. They have a hard covering on the outside of their bodies. _____ _____

3. They do not have bones inside their bodies. _____ _____

4. They use their front legs to keep themselves clean. _____ _____

5. Eggs are laid underground. _____ _____

6. Shorthorns are the kind we see most often. _____ _____

7. Longhorns have long feelers and like to move at night. _____ _____

8. Some of the insects may eat farmland crops. _____ _____

9. It is warmer in the summertime than it is in the winter. _____ _____

10. They may be found in your backyard or in an empty lot. _____ _____

Add two words together to make one compound word.

Mark's Surprise

Characters in stories want you to listen to them. In this lesson, you will learn to know when a character is speaking. You will read about a boy who gets surprised.

 ## KEYS to Dialogue

Words spoken aloud are called dialogue.

LEARN   When someone in a story is speaking out loud, the words the character says are called dialogue. Two clues can help you find dialogue. One clue is words like <u>said</u>, <u>told</u>, and <u>asked</u>. Quotation marks are the other clue. They look like this: " ". Words between quotation marks are dialogue.

DIRECTIONS Underline the dialogue in the sentences.

A. "Look at the dragon kite in the sky!" yelled Gary.

B. Sandy asked, "May I please have some milk?"

 ## Practice With Dialogue

DIRECTIONS Read the sentence. Color the picture of the person who is speaking.

1. "It's time for dinner, Joey," called Mother.

DIRECTIONS Read the story. Pay attention to the dialogue.

"Mark, come over here!" called Tina.

Mark ran over to see what Tina was looking at.

"What is it?" he asked.

"Come and see what I found in the grass," Tina whispered.

"Tina, it's only an old rock," Mark told her.

"Look again!" giggled Tina.

Mark came closer. He bent over the rock. Suddenly it started to move.

"Okay, Tina," Mark muttered. "What's the trick?"

"It's no trick," Tina answered.

Slowly a head peeked out from the rock.

"It's not a rock. It's a turtle," laughed Mark. "You sure fooled me, Tina!"

DIRECTIONS Put a check on the line before each sentence that is dialogue.

_____ 1. "Come and see what I found in the grass."

_____ 2. "It's a turtle."

_____ 3. Mark came closer.

_____ 4. "What is it?"

_____ 5. Slowly a head peeked out from the rock.

REMEMBER Characters speak to you through dialogue.

Greetings!

It's fun to get cards. The people who send them want you to do what the cards say. When you do school work, you do what the directions say. In this lesson, you will read about greeting cards. You will learn about following directions.

 ## KEYS to Following Directions

Read! Think! Do! Check!

LEARN Following directions can be easy if you practice good habits.

1. READ carefully.
2. THINK about what to do.
3. DO one step at a time.
4. CHECK your work.

DIRECTIONS When Joey got chicken pox, Joey's friends missed him. They made him a card. Look at the card and follow the directions.

1. Circle the telescope in the top right corner.

2. What do you see in the middle of the card?

_____

3. Put an X on the binoculars in the bottom left corner.

4. What do you see in the upper left corner?

_____

5. Which corner are the eyeglasses in?

_____

Hope to
see you soon!

DIRECTIONS Follow the directions to show what the card Terry sent to Joey looked like.

1. Draw a gray cloud in the top left corner.

2. Draw an umbrella in the bottom right corner.

3. Print get well on the line in the middle of the card.

4. Draw seven raindrops in the top right corner.

5. Draw a pair of rain boots in the bottom left corner.

The sun won't shine until you

_____

DIRECTIONS Some of Joey's friends bought cards at Mailer's card shop. Mr. Mailer keeps his cards in groups on the shelf. Look at the picture on his shelf. Follow the directions.

1. Print the correct name for each group of cards on the line above the shelf.

2. Draw one more card in the group on the right. Be sure it is the right kind of card.

3. Circle the group of cards in the middle.

4. Color three cards in the group on the left.

Read and Apply

DIRECTIONS Read the story. Help Joey mail his card.

While he was home, Joey got many get well cards. One of the cards was from his grandmother. Grandma wrote a note on her card. She told Joey some good news.

"Grandma has a new job," Joey called to his mother. "She will be working in a tall office building in the city. I'm so proud of Grandma. I'm going to send her a card to tell her how glad I am."

When Joey was well again, he went to Mailer's Card Shop. He asked Mr. Mailer to help him find a card for Grandma. Mr. Mailer found a card that said "Congratulations."

"That long word means you are happy about someone's good news," said Mr. Mailer.

"Then that's the card for me," replied Joey.

Joey ran home from the card shop. He wanted to get his card to the mailbox before the mail carrier picked up the mail.

"I want Grandma to get this tomorrow," said Joey.

He quickly wrote a note on the card. He put in a picture of himself with the chicken pox, too.

"Oh, no," said Joey. "I only have ten minutes to get this card to the mailbox. Mom, will you help me address this envelope?"

Joey's mother wrote down the steps for Joey to follow to send the card to Grandma's office. Joey had only five minutes left. He raced through the directions. Then he dashed to the mailbox and dropped the card through the slot.

"Great! I made it just in time," exclaimed Joey.

For the next few days, Joey waited for an answer from Grandma. Finally, he got an envelope that looked like a greeting card.

"Oh, no," said Joey, after he looked at the envelope. "This is the same card I sent to Grandma."

Joey's mother looked at the envelope.

"Joey," she said. "The post office could not deliver your card. They had to send it back. You did not follow directions carefully."

"I guess I was in too much of a hurry," Joey said glumly. "Can we try again with a new envelope? This time I will be more careful."

DIRECTIONS Help Joey redo the envelope by following the directions carefully.

<u>Joey's Address</u>
Joey Blum
24 Elm Street
Boston, MA 12345

<u>Grandma's Office Address</u>
Tower Incorporated
152 Broad Avenue
New York, NY 54321

1. Write Joey's address in the top left corner.

2. Write Grandma's office address in the middle.

3. Write ATTN: Betty Downs in the bottom left corner.

4. Draw a postage stamp in the top right corner.

REMEMBER Read! Think! Do! Check!

A Fish Story

You can't remember everything you read. You <u>can</u> remember the important ideas.

In this lesson, you will learn to find important ideas when you read. You will read about fish as pets.

 ## KEYS to Main Ideas and Details

Main ideas are important ideas. Details tell more.

LEARN The main idea tells a what a whole paragraph is about. Details tell more about the main idea.

DIRECTIONS Read the paragraph. Underline the main idea sentence.

Gold fish make good pets. They are easy to care for. They don't cost too much. They are fun to watch.

 ## Practice With Main Ideas and Details

DIRECTIONS Circle the number of each detail that could tell more about the main idea.

1. Dogs make good pets.

2. Cats make good pets.

3. Fish don't eat much.

4. Fish don't take much space.

DIRECTIONS Read the story. Answer the questions.

Trish peered through the window of Jenkins' Pet Store. No customers were in the store. Trish decided to go in.

"What can I do for you?" said Mr. Jenkins.

"I need to know about fish," Trish said. "I asked for a fish tank. Dad says I should find out about taking care of fish. Then if I still want them, I can have them."

Mr. Jenkins walked around the pet store with her. He showed her the different kinds of fish.

"Fish are easier than dogs or cats," he said. "They do need care, though. They need to be fed every day. They need a clean aquarium. They need plants and rocks to hide in.

"Fish are worth the work. They are pretty and fun to watch. Let me know what you decide. I'll help you pick some out."

As Trish rode her bike home, she smiled. Her dad would be glad she had learned so much. She had made up her mind. She could take good care of her fish.

DIRECTIONS Answer the questions.

1. Circle the letter of the best title.
   a. Learning About Fish
   b. No Fish Today

2. Fill in the blanks to complete the details.
   a. Mr. Jenkins owns the

   _____ _____.

   b. The fish can hide in

   _____ and _____.

   c. Fish need to be fed

   _____.

REMEMBER Main ideas and details help you know what you read.

Some Cold, Hard Facts

Snow that falls in the mountains doesn't always melt in the spring. Each year new snow falls. The snow turns to ice. A glacier is born.

In this lesson, you will learn more about glaciers. You will also learn about main ideas and details.

KEYS to Main Ideas

Find the important idea. The details tell more about it.

LEARN Every paragraph you read has one big idea. That big idea is its main idea. Other sentences tell more about the main idea. They are called details.

DIRECTIONS Read the paragraph. The main idea sentence has been left out. Circle the number of the sentence that tells the main idea. Write the sentence on the line.

A glacier that covers large parts of the land is called an icecap. Some glaciers run downhill like a river. They are called valley glaciers. When valley glaciers spill out of the mountains and spread out, they are called piedmont glaciers.

1. Glaciers are made of ice and snow.

2. There are many different kinds of glaciers.

3. Rivers can turn into glaciers.

2 Practice With Details

DIRECTIONS Read each paragraph. The main idea sentence is in dark print. Fill in the blanks to complete the details.

A. Glaciers do not look like they are moving, but they are. They move so slowly we cannot measure their movement in miles. We measure their movement in inches per day. The top of the glacier moves faster than the bottom. The bottom moves more slowly because it drags against the ground. This makes the glacier change shape. It gets huge cracks and rough spots.

1. Glaciers move very

   _____.

2. Glaciers change

   _____.

3. Glaciers get huge

   _____and rough

   _____.

B. Glaciers can change the shape of the earth. They dig out huge valleys. They drop tons of rock in large piles. Glaciers can scrape away the soil as they move. They polish the rocks and mark them with deep scratches. Today we can look at the land and see where glaciers have been. The Great Lakes were made by glaciers.

1. Glaciers dig out huge

   _____.

2. Glaciers drop large piles of

   _____.

3. Glaciers made the

   _____.

3 Read and Apply

DIRECTIONS Poems can have main ideas and details, too. Read the poems. Then write the letter of the correct answer to each question on the line.

When All the World Is Full of Snow

I never know
just where to go,
when all the world
is full of snow.

I do not want
to make a track,
not even
to the shed and back.

I only want
to watch and wait,
while snow moths settle
on the gate,

and swarming frost flakes
fill the trees
with billions
of albino bees.

I only want
myself to be
as silent as
a winter tree,

to hear the swirling
stillness grow,
when all the world
is full of snow.

—N.M. Bodecker

1. The author wants to tell about _____ when it snows hard.

    a. how it feels
    b. how to play
    c. where to walk

2. Snowflakes on the gate look like _____ .

    a. white birds
    b. white leaves
    c. white moths

3. The author does not like to make _____ in the smooth snow.

    a. snow angels
    b. tracks
    c. pictures

First Snow

Snow makes whiteness where it falls.
The bushes look like popcorn balls.
And places where I always play,
Look like somewhere else today.

1. This poem tells about how it _____ when it snows.

    a. feels
    b. smells
    c. looks

2. Bushes look like _____ .

    a. popcorn balls
    b. baseballs
    c. footballs

3. Familiar places can look _____ after a snowfall.

    a. colder
    b. different
    c. darker

REMEMBER Details tell more about important ideas.

A Puppet Play

Think of the last time you made a project. Were there steps to follow? Did it turn out the way you hoped it would?

In this lesson, you will read about a puppet play. You will see how important it is to follow steps in the right order.

 ## KEYS to the Right Order

Which step comes first?

LEARN You can't read a book until you open it up. You would look silly if you put your shoes on before your socks. When you read, it is important to pay attention to correct order, too.

DIRECTIONS Lillie and Franco decided to make treats for the play. They found a recipe. They found everything they needed. Then they looked at the directions. They didn't make sense. Help Lillie and Franco. Number the steps to put them in the right order.

Yummie Crunchies	Directions:
2 cups of powdered sugar ½ cup of peanut butter 1 beaten egg 1 tablespoon of butter ½ teaspoon of vanilla ½ cup of sunflower seeds	_____ Roll balls in seeds. _____ Mix the first five things together. _____ Chill four to five hours. _____ Shape into balls.

DIRECTIONS Read the story. Circle the letter of the correct answer.

Jim and Barb wanted music during the play. They decided to make their own musical instruments.

"Let's make a shoebox guitar and a tambourine," said Barb.

"That's a great idea," said Jim. "How do you make them?"

"It's easy," answered Barb. "For a guitar we need a shoebox with a lid, scissors, some tape, and some rubber bands in different sizes. Then we just need to get the steps in the right order."

Jim found everything he needed. Then he made the guitar while Barb told him what to do.

"First cut a round hole in the top of the box," she said. "Tape the lid to the box. Then stretch the rubber bands around the box. You can tape a ruler to the top for a handle if you want to."

While Jim made the guitar, Barb made the tambourine. She

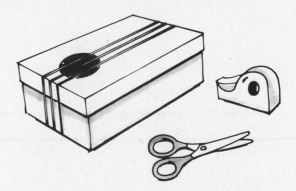

found two paper plates, some beans, and some crayons. She borrowed the tape from Jim.

First she colored bright patterns on the bottoms of the plates. Then she put the beans on the bottom plate and taped the top plate to it. Barb liked the sound it made when she shook it.

"This is great!" said Jim. "Let's make some music."

1. What should you do first to make a guitar?
   a. Go to the music store.
   b. Get a shoebox with a lid.

2. What do you do after you put the beans on the plate?
   a. Tape the plates together.
   b. Put rubber bands around it.

3. What extra step can you add to the guitar?
   a. Add a ruler for a handle.
   b. Tape beans to the plate.

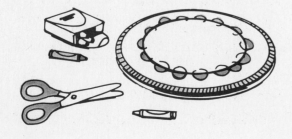

Read and Apply

DIRECTIONS Read the story. Number the sentences to put them in order.

After the boys and girls planned treats and music, they began to plan their puppet play.

"This play about a king, a princess, and a troll is really funny," said Bud. "Let's make the puppets, then practice our lines."

"I'll be the king," said Stanley.

He drew a picture of a king on stiff cardboard. He cut out the shape. Then he pasted on a real cloth robe. He made a crown of shiny foil. Finally, Stanley taped a straw on the back for a handle. The king was ready to speak.

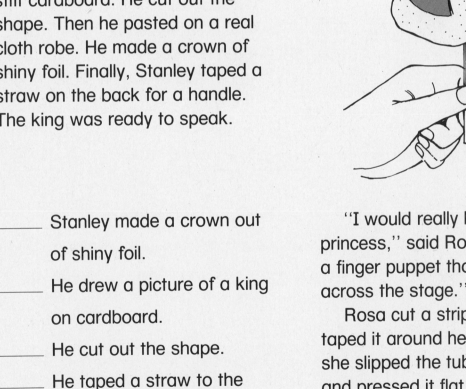

_____ Stanley made a crown out of shiny foil.

_____ He drew a picture of a king on cardboard.

_____ He cut out the shape.

_____ He taped a straw to the back of the puppet.

_____ Stanley pasted on a real cloth robe.

"I would really like to be the princess," said Rosa. "I will make a finger puppet that can glide across the stage."

Rosa cut a strip of paper. She taped it around her finger. Then she slipped the tube off her finger and pressed it flat. Rosa drew a face and a beautiful gown on the paper. She spread glitter all over the gown."

"Now my princess will make the children's eyes sparkle," Rosa said.

_____ Rosa taped the paper around her finger.

_____ Rosa cut a strip of paper.

_____ She slipped the tube off and pressed it flat.

_____ Rosa spread glitter on the gown.

_____ She drew on a face and a beautiful gown.

"Rosa's puppet is pretty," said Vera, "but I want my troll puppet to be scary."

She colored a picture of a scary green troll on stiff cardboard. She drew two circles near the bottom. Vera cut out the puppet. Then she cut out the circles. Vera glued on bits of yarn for crazy hair. She put her first and second fingers through the holes to make the troll walk. Vera walked her troll across the table toward the king and princess.

"Now my troll can run after the other puppets," laughed Vera. "Look out!"

Stanley and Rosa made their puppets scream. They all laughed.

_____ Vera cut out the puppet.

_____ She drew two circles near the bottom of her puppet.

_____ Vera colored a scary green troll on cardboard.

_____ She cut the circles out.

_____ She glued on bits of yarn for hair.

REMEMBER Do steps in the right order, and the things you make will turn out to be great.

When School Is Out

There are so many things to do after school, on weekends, or in the summer. In this lesson, you will read about things some boys and girls do when school is out. You will learn how things happen in a special order.

KEYS to the Right Sequence

The order things happen in is their sequence.

LEARN Things in a story happen in a certain order. We call this order the sequence. Words like first, then, next, finally, and last are hints about sequence. Read the sentences below. The underlined words tell the order, or sequence, of what happened.

EXAMPLE First I put on my swimming suit. Then I jumped into the water.

DIRECTIONS Underline the sequence words in each pair of sentences.

1. The first stop in our tour of the museum was the mummy room.
   Then we saw the dinosaur bones.

2. The pilot climbed into the airplane before the passengers arrived.
   At last, the plane was ready to take off.

3. First you put a quarter in the machine.
   Then you can play the game.

DIRECTIONS Read the pairs of sentences. Write 1 on the line before the sentence that comes first. Write 2 before the sentence that comes next.

1. _____ Eddie ran to first base.

   _____ Eddie hit the baseball first.

2. _____ Next Tammy paddled down the river.

   _____ Tammy stepped into the canoe.

3. _____ Then Mickey pulled up the covers.

   _____ Mickey climbed into bed.

4. _____ Nancy bought her ticket.

   _____ Then she rode the train to Grandma's.

5. _____ It started to rain harder.

   _____ Mandy finally put up her umbrella.

6. _____ The last thing he did was paint the fence.

   _____ Dad worked in the yard all day.

7. _____ First Andy plugged in the computer.

   _____ Then he turned it on.

8. _____ Jim and Mary filled the bathtub.

   _____ Next they had to find the dog.

DIRECTIONS Read the story. Answer the questions.

When Randy woke up, he remembered it was Saturday. Saturday was always a busy day. This Saturday would be busier than ever. At first, he just wanted to stay in bed. After his mother called him three times, he finally got up. Then he started to look forward to his busy day.

After breakfast, Randy grabbed his trumpet. His first stop would be his music lesson. Randy had practiced every evening after dinner. He was eager to play his new song for his teacher.

Then it was time for his trip to the dentist. Randy wasn't looking forward to that, but he wanted his teeth to stay healthy. Finally that was over. He didn't have any cavities! Now he knew that the rest of the day would be fun.

Before he could go to his club's car wash, he raced home for lunch. Then it was time to hop on his bike. He hurried to the gas station on the corner. He and his friends washed car after car. Sometimes they got wet. They had fun all the time.

Randy knew the best part of the day was coming next. After dinner, he was going out with his big brother. His brother was going to take him to the circus. It was the last thing on his schedule, and it would be the best.

The circus started with a huge parade. First came the elephants. Next came the clowns. Finally, the ringmaster rode in on a tall black horse. The show was about to start.

After that busy day, Randy was ready for bed.

"I'm glad it was Saturday," he said to himself. "It's good to have a nice relaxing day away from school."

DIRECTIONS Choose the word that fits best in each sentence. Write it on the line.

1. _____ Randy could go to the car wash, he had to go to the dentist.

   a. Before   **b.** After   **c.** Then

2. He went to the car wash _____ he went to the circus.

   a. after   **b.** then   **c.** before

3. _____ it was time for bed.

   a. Before   **b.** Finally   **c.** First

4. The best part of Randy's day was coming _____ .

   a. next   **b.** before   **c.** first

5. The _____ person in the parade was the ringmaster.

   a. first   **b.** finally   **c.** last

6. After being called three times, Randy _____ got out of bed.

   a. before   **b.** first   **c.** finally

7. The _____ thing on his schedule would be the best.

   a. last   **b.** first   **c.** then

8. _____ that busy day, Randy was ready for bed.

   a. Finally   **b.** After   **c.** Before

REMEMBER Sequence means order.

Beware of Bears

Sometimes answers are easy to find. The words you need are right on the page. Sometimes you have to figure the answer out yourself. You have to think hard and look for clues.

In this lesson, you will practice looking for clues. You will read about teddy bears.

KEYS to Finding Clues

Look at words on the page. Use what you already know.

LEARN Some questions are easy to answer. The answers are right in the sentence.

A. E. J. Bear put on his jacket and walked out the door.

1. What did E. J. put on? _____

Sometimes the answers are not in the sentences. Then you need to look for clues in the words. You need to think, too.

B. E. J. Bear put on his jacket and walked out the door. Fluffy, white snow had fallen during the night. E. J. wished he had put on his cap and mittens, too.
"I should have known better," thought E. J.

1. What season of the year is it? _____

2. How did you know? _____

2 Practice Finding Clues

DIRECTIONS Be a detective. As you read the story, look for clues to help you answer the questions.

A. The day of the picnic was finally here. Susie wanted to wear her new striped shoelaces in her sneakers. She looked in the shoebox. The laces were missing.

"Oh, no!" cried Susie. "Where could they be?"

Susie looked in her gym bag. She looked in her closet. The laces weren't anywhere. Susie decided to try the car.

On her way outside, Susie passed the shelf where she kept her biggest teddy bear. She glanced at the shelf. When she saw Teddy Budd's shoes, she started to laugh.

1. Where did Susie find her shoelaces?

B. "I want to play with the red truck," said Annie Bear to her little brother Benjie.

"You can't have it," snarled the smaller bear. "It's mine. Daddy bought it for me. Play with your own cars."

"Then I won't play with you at all," said Annie. "You should learn to share your toys."

Benjie stomped into the kitchen and began to cry.

"Now I'm all alone," he sobbed to Daddy. "What can I do?"

"It's hard to share new toys," Daddy said. "Let's find Annie and talk about it."

1. How did Benjie feel when Annie left?

DIRECTIONS Read each story. Use clues to help you answer the questions. Tell what clues you used.

A. "This toy store is a busy place," thought Mikey Bear. "I sure hope someone buys me today."

Mikey sat up straight. He held his furry ears high. He puffed out his chest so his little green vest would look just right.

Soon a little boy and his mother walked through the door.

"That's just the bear I want," said the boy. He pointed to the bear right next to Mikey. Mikey's heart fell right to the bottom of his vest. He was afraid he would cry.

"That's a good choice," said the mother. "I think we'll get the teddy bear beside him, too. Gina will just love the little bear in the green vest."

Mikey didn't feel like crying anymore. He thought he would burst.

1. Why did Mikey stop crying?

_____

_____

2. What words in the story helped you answer question 1?

_____

_____

3. What did you already know that helped you answer the question?

_____

_____

B. Brenda Bear woke up from her nap. She yawned and stretched her arms high.

"I'm starving," she said, as she padded toward the kitchen.

She opened the cupboard door and lifted down a large, brown pot. The letters on the pot had rubbed off over the years. All she could read was the beginning of the letter H.

Brenda Bear smiled. She couldn't wait for her snack. She took the lid off the pot. Then she dipped her paw inside.

What a bad surprise! Her paw didn't come out of the pot sticky like it usually did. She poked her nose into the pot. It was empty.

"Oh, well," sighed Brenda Bear. "I guess it's time to make a trip to the old bee tree."

Brenda picked up the pot and walked out the door.

1. What is usually in the pot?

_____

2. What words in the story helped you answer question 1?

_____

_____

3. What did you already know that helped you answer the question?

_____

4. What was Brenda Bear going out to do?

_____

_____

5. What words in the story helped you answer question 4?

_____

_____

6. What did you already know that helped you answer the question?

_____

_____

REMEMBER Think when you read.

All About Dogs

A good reader must also be a good detective. You search for clues to understand what you read. In this lesson, you will learn about gathering clues. You will use the clues to learn about dogs.

 ## KEYS to Gathering Clues

Use ideas from the story with ideas from your head.

LEARN Sometimes a story doesn't tell you everything in words. You must figure things out for yourself. These questions will help you.

1. What clues can I find in the story?
2. What do I already know about the ideas in the story?

DIRECTIONS Read the story. Gather clues that tell what kind of snack they are making. Answer the questions.

Eric and Brian were hungry. They decided to go to Eric's for a snack.

Eric got down a pan, some oil and a salt shaker. Then he found a large snack bowl.

"It won't take long to make this," Eric said, as he took a glass jar from the shelf.

"Great. That's my favorite snack," answered Brian.

1. What kind of snack did the boys make? _____

2. Underline the words in the story that helped answer question 1.

3. List the ideas from your own mind that helped. _____

DIRECTIONS Read the short stories and answer the questions. Then list the best clues you used to answer each question.

Heather and Gabe were busy in the kitchen. They had already mixed the batter. Then they rolled the dough flat. Next they took turns cutting out stars, trees, and circles. Soon, the shapes were baking in the oven.

Annie held Muffy on her lap. Muffy was covered with mud. A tub of warm water was sitting nearby on the grass. Next to the tub stood an old bench. On the bench were some soap, a soft brush, and a big fluffy towel. Soon, John came out the door with a leash. The children put the leash on Muffy's collar and walked to the tub.

I. What were Heather and Gabe baking?

_____

2. List the clues from the story.

_____

3. List the clues from your own mind.

_____

I. What were Annie and John going to do to Muffy?

_____

2. List the clues from the story.

_____

3. List the clues from your own mind.

3 Read and Apply

DIRECTIONS You have learned about dogs by being around them, reading dog stories, and seeing them in movies and on television. Think about what you already know about dogs. Write two ideas about dogs under each heading.

Why People Own Dogs

_____

_____

Things Dogs Need

_____

_____

What Dogs Need

_____

_____

Names for Pet Dogs

_____

_____

Ways Dogs Move

_____

_____

Kinds of Dogs

_____

_____

DIRECTIONS Read the story about the day Nan got her new pet. Use the clues in the story with the clues in your mind to answer the questions.

The first thing Nan did when she got her new pet was to take him to the vet. After Dr. Cohen checked Bo over, she gave Nan a list of things to do.

1. Feed him good food and water every day.
2. Give him something safe to chew on.

3. Make him a clean sleeping box or a warm house.
4. Brush his coat every day.
5. Be sure to let him walk and run outdoors.
6. Play with him.

When she finished reading the list, Nan smiled.

"I will be happy to do everything on the list," she promised, "especially number six."

1. Is Bo a turtle?

_____

What were your clues?

_____

2. Is Bo a goldfish?

_____

What were your clues?

_____

3. What kind of pet is Bo?

_____

What were your clues?

_____

4. Does Bo have long or short hair?

_____

What were your clues?

_____

5. Will Nan take good care of Bo?

_____

What were your clues?

_____

REMEMBER Use what you know to help you learn more.

Using Clues

Words on the page and ideas in your head work together when you read. You need both kinds of clues to understand what you're reading.

In this lesson, you will practice using clues to understand what you read.

 ## KEYS to Using Clues to Find Answers

Put your ideas to work when you read.

LEARN The more you know about a subject, the easier it is to read about it. You can use what you already know to fill in ideas the words don't tell you.

DIRECTIONS Use all your clues to find the answer to the riddle.

I have one eye,
But I can't see.
People can sew
Nice things with me.
⠀⠀⠀What am I?

I am a _____

② Practice Using Clues

DIRECTIONS Read each riddle. Underline words that give you clues to the answer. Draw a picture to answer the riddle.

1. Slice me or squeeze

   I'm good just the same.

   If you guess my color,

   Then you'll know my name.   I am an _____.

2. I have big round wheels.

   I'm bright as can be.

   I'm ready to go.

   Will you pedal me?   I am a _____.

3. Green in the summer,

   Brown in the fall.

   If you use a rake,

   You'll get us all.   We are _____.

4. I have many teeth,

   But I never bite.

   Use me or a brush

   Each morning and night.   I am a _____.

Read and Apply

DIRECTIONS Read each story. Answer the questions. Write your clues on the lines.

A. Matthew had been watching them build the new home all spring. He could look right down at it from his bedroom window. He was really excited when he first spotted the light blue eggs.

One day when Matthew woke up, he heard a new sound. It was a soft, squeaky noise that sounded like "Cheep! Cheep!" Matthew tiptoed to the window. He already knew what he would find.

He was looking right down into a nest of tiny open beaks. As he watched, a larger bird flew up to the nest. It had a dark back and a reddish-orange stomach.

Matthew ran out into the hall and called out to his family.

"They're here! They're here. The new babies are here!"

1. What kind of babies did Matthew find?

_____

2. List the clues you found in the words on the page.

_____

_____

_____

3. List the clues you already had in your head.

_____

_____

B. Eric walked into the garage carrying a brown paper bag. His sister Jackie looked at him curiously. He was holding the bag so carefully. Jackie wondered what he had found this time.

"What do you have in that bag?" Jackie demanded.

"I won't tell you," Eric teased. "I have something special, but you'll have to guess what it is."

"Okay," said Jackie. "Give me some clues."

"Well," Eric said, "there's a kind of container inside this bag."

"Is there something alive in it?" Jackie asked.

"It is alive, but it's not moving around. In fact, it's sort of asleep."

"When it wakes up, will it be friendly?" Jackie asked.

Eric laughed.

"It's not unfriendly," he answered. "I mean, it won't bite or anything."

"I bet it's an ugly bug," she said. "I know you like them."

"You're partly right," said Eric. "It's not ugly. Soon it will be beautiful. When it comes out of its cocoon, you will like it. When it flies away, you will miss it."

1. What will come out of Eric's cocoon?

   _____

   _____

2. List the clues you found in the on the page.

   _____

   _____

   _____

3. List the clues you already had in your head.

   _____

   _____

   _____

REMEMBER Make your own ideas work for you.

Super Cats

Have you ever heard of a hero cat? *Buffet Cat Club News* has. The magazine held a contest to choose a cat hero of the year.

In this lesson, you will read about hero cats. You will learn about making predictions.

KEYS to Making Predictions

What will happen next?

LEARN When you read, it's fun to guess what will happen next. Think about what you have already read. Then make your best guess about what will happen.

DIRECTIONS Cover the bottom of this page with a piece of paper. Then read the story. Write your prediction. Then read the ending.

You know you should be careful around electricity. Sweetie Pie the cat knows it, too.

One day Sweetie Pie was resting on her window sill. A neighbor girl was playing nearby. No one else was around. Suddenly, Sweetie Pie's friend was in big trouble. She had touched a live wire. The current held her. She couldn't let go of the wire.

What did Sweetie Pie do? _____

_____

Quick as a flash, Sweetie Pie jumped from her window sill perch. She jumped right onto her friend's hand and knocked it from the wire. Thanks to Sweetie Pie, her neighbor's life was saved.

DIRECTIONS Read the statements. Make a prediction. Circle the letter of the sentence that will happen next.

1. Alan lives in an apartment.
   Alan wants a pet.
   a. Alan will get a St. Bernard dog.
   b. Alan will not get a pet.
   c. Alan will buy some goldfish.

2. Janie has an extra ticket to a baseball game.
   Janie's cousin loves baseball.
   a. Janie will invite her cousin to the game.
   b. Janie will go alone to the game.
   c. Janie's cousin will get a job as an umpire.

3. Rafe has a test in math tomorrow.
   Rafe has studied all his math facts.
   a. Rafe will fail the math test.
   b. Rafe will pass the math test.
   c. Rafe will pass the spelling test.

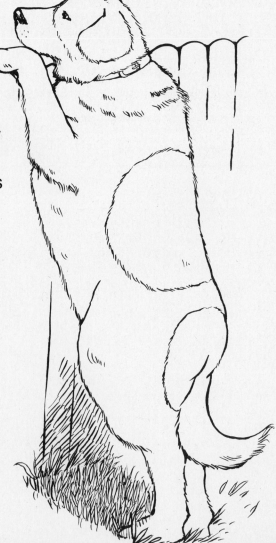

4. Our school's soccer team has won every game.
   We are playing against a school who has lost every game.
   a. Our team will probably win the game.
   b. Our team will probably lose the game.
   c. Our teams will probably tie.

5. Alice's sister has a birthday next week.
   Alice has only saved fifty cents.
   a. Alice will buy a TV for her sister.
   b. Alice will not give her sister a present.
   c. Alice will make her sister a present.

Read and Apply

DIRECTIONS Now try some more predictions. Cover the page. Read the story. Make your prediction. Then read the ending.

A. Baby's owner had had a hard day at work. As soon as she came home, she started dinner. Then she sat down to read her newspaper. Baby's owner didn't realize just how tired she was. As soon as she started to read, she fell asleep.

What will happen next? _____

_____

_____

The next thing she knew, her cat was jumping on her stomach. Baby's owner tried to go back to sleep. Baby wouldn't let her. Baby jumped on her again. He cried and meowed.

Suddenly Baby's owner was wide awake. She had finally noticed that her house was filled with dark black smoke. She ran to the kitchen.

What will happen next? _____

_____

_____

In the kitchen, she found that the house wasn't on fire. The food was. The pan was melting. Quickly she turned off the stove. She opened the window to get rid of the smoke. If Baby's owner had slept longer, a bad fire could have started.

Was Baby's owner grateful? You bet she was. So were her other pets—eighteen more cats and two dogs!

B. Would you hire a cat for a babysitter? A cat named Smokey could do the job. He already has some good experience.

One day Mrs. Oliver put her youngest son to bed for his nap. Ronnie didn't want a nap. He wanted to play. Finally Mrs. Oliver thought he was asleep. She went to the yard to work in the garden.

"Take good care of Ronnie," she told Smokey.

What will happen next? _____

_____

_____

As she worked in her garden, Mrs. Oliver heard a noise at the back door. Smokey was clawing at the screen and crying.

"Bad cat!" she said. "Go away from the door."

Smokey wouldn't go away. He kept scratching and making noise. Mrs. Oliver was getting angry. She put down her spade. The minute she opened the door Smokey raced away. He ran right to Ronnie's room. Then he ran back. He howled and ran down the hall again.

What will happen next? _____

_____

_____

This time Mrs. Oliver followed. Ronnie was choking. He had swallowed a small piece from one of his games. Mrs. Oliver removed the game piece quickly. Ronnie stopped choking.

Now Smokey has a job in the Oliver home. Every night before he goes to sleep, Smokey checks on all the children.

REMEMBER It's fun to make predictions as you read.

Why Did It Happen?

Things that we do make other things happen. If you leave a skate on the stairs, someone will fall. If you take good care of your kitten, it will love you. In this lesson, you will learn to find out why things happen in the stories you read. You will solve a mystery.

 ## KEYS to Cause and Effect

An effect is what happens. The cause makes it happen.

LEARN To find the effect, ask "What happened?" To find the cause, ask "Why did it happen?"

DIRECTIONS The large picture shows something that happened, or the effect. Find the picture that shows the cause. Color it.

A.

B.

C.

D.

② Practice With Cause and Effect

DIRECTIONS Look at each picture. Circle the letter of the sentence that tells what caused the event in the picture to happen.

1.

    a. Rags chewed up Phil's sneaker.
    b. Rags learned a good trick.
    c. Rags and Mom went for a walk.

2.

    a. It is a bright, sunny day.
    b. Dad is going to stay inside.
    c. It is raining hard.

3.

    a. Lee struck out.
    b. Lee hit a home run.
    c. Lee dropped the ball.

4.

    a. Pat is very hungry.
    b. Pat doesn't like apples.
    c. Pat is not hungry now.

5.

    a. The baby has a new toy.
    b. The baby has nothing to play with.
    c. The baby is happy.

DIRECTIONS Read the story. Think about why things happened.

Jerry opened his eyes. The first thing he saw was the calendar hanging on the back of his door. Today's date was circled in red.

"Oh, boy," said Jeremy. "My birthday is finally here."

Jeremy was happy. It felt good to be older. Today he would finally be allowed to ride his bike to the park by himself.

He had to add one more chore to his list. That was okay, though. One more chore meant a bigger allowance.

Jeremy hurried to get dressed. Something strange was happening. He pulled on his socks. He tugged and tugged, but they would not stay up. Then he had to squeeze his feet into his shoes.

When Jeremy looked in the mirror, he saw that his jeans were too short. His ankles stuck out. When he lifted his arms to comb his hair, his tee shirt came up, too. He could see his stomach.

"What is wrong?" Jeremy thought. "Did Mom shrink all my clothes? How could she shrink my shoes? This is a mystery. Did someone sneak in and take my

real clothes while I was asleep?"

Mom called down the hall. It was time for breakfast.

"Mom," Jeremy whined. "Something is wrong with my clothes."

Mom looked at Jeremy. She laughed.

"Your clothes didn't shrink," she said. "Have you forgotten what day it is? You are getting older. You are also getting bigger. Today after school we will shop for some clothes that will fit a boy your age."

DIRECTIONS Think about the story you just read. Read the sentences that tell about things that happened in the story. Write the cause for each effect on the line.

1. The date on the calendar was circled in red.

   _____

2. Jeremy would be allowed to ride to the park by himself.

   _____

3. Jeremy would get a bigger allowance.

   _____

   _____

4. Jeremy's ankles stuck out from under his jeans.

   _____

5. All of Jeremy's clothes were too small.

   _____

6. Jeremy and Mom will go shopping after school.

   _____

REMEMBER Things happen because something made them happen.

Wilderness Friends

It would be strange if everyone looked just alike. We wouldn't be able to tell each other apart. It's a good thing people, plants, animals, and other things are different in some ways.

In this lesson, you will learn to compare and contrast. You will read about two people who seemed very different, but found they were alike in many ways.

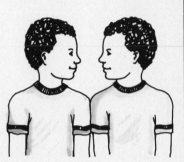

 ## KEYS to Comparing and Contrasting

Compare to find how things are alike.
Contrast to find their differences.

EXAMPLE   Compare and contrast oranges and lemons.
Compare: Oranges and lemons are both fruits.
Contrast: Oranges are orange. Lemons are yellow.

DIRECTIONS   Look at the pictures. Read each phrase. If the phrase tells about the picture, write its number on the line.

1. has feathers   4. swims in the water

2. lives out of doors   5. has fur

3. can be bigger than a pony   6. has large paws

A. _____   **B.** _____   **C.** _____

Compare/Contrast **79**

② Practice Comparing and Contrasting

DIRECTIONS Here's a chance for you to compare. Think of things that will fit in each group. The things in each group will be alike in at least one way.

A. Things with Legs

_____

_____

_____

B. Animals Smaller Than a Cat

_____

_____

_____

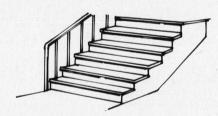

C. Things You Can Use to Go Up

_____

_____

_____

D. Things You Can Ride

_____

_____

_____

DIRECTIONS Now it's time to contrast. Put words from the lists you made into two different groups.

E. Things That Are Alive

_____

_____

_____

F. Things That Are Not Alive

_____

_____

_____

DIRECTIONS Read the story. Look for ways the boys in the story are alike. Look for ways they are different.

In 1820 Black Eagle was eight years old. That was the year his father gave him a pony. He chose a black pony. It had a white star on its forehead. He called the pony White Star.

The pony was not just for fun. With a pony, Black Eagle could learn to hunt and help take care of his family.

Black Eagle learned to hunt. He rode many days with the hunters. On other days, Black Eagle and White Star went to the bank of the river. Black Eagle would fish and swim. He was the best swimmer in his tribe. He had won many races.

Black Eagle had to learn many things. His father taught him to speak other Native American languages. He learned about special days and customs. He learned to work with the others to make a good life for the whole tribe. Black Eagle was a good student.

In the same year, another eight-year-old boy settled in Black Eagle's neighborhood. His family had traveled hundreds of miles to settle in this land. His name was Eli. Eli knew many things, too. He knew how to read and write. He knew how to do arithmetic. He didn't know how to live in the wilderness. Eli knew he would learn soon.

Eli's father gave him a pony. The pony was black. It had a white streak down the middle of its forehead. Eli named it Blaze. Blaze and Eli helped with his family's work. There were many new jobs for Eli. Land had to be cleared. A house had to be built. Eli learned to hunt for food.

One day Eli and Blaze went to the river bank. On the other side of the bank stood Black Eagle and White Star. They stared at each other. The boys looked very different, but they were both lonely. Each boy wanted a friend. Black Eagle swam across the river. That was the beginning of a friendship that would last many years.

Both boys liked to hunt and fish. They liked to play games and ride their ponies. Each boy knew some things that the other wanted to know. Black Eagle and Eli learned each other's language. Eli taught Black Eagle to read and write. Black Eagle taught Eli to live closely with nature. They learned each other's customs.

As the years went by, the boys grew into young men. They were still friends. Then one day Black Eagle came to tell Eli he was taking his family to another part of the wilderness. Eli said goodbye to his friend. They both wondered if they would ever see each other again. They knew they would always remember.

DIRECTIONS Write **T** on the line if the statement is true.

	Black Eagle	Eli
I. His father gave him a pony.	_____	_____
2. He won swimming races.	_____	_____
3. His family was new to the wilderness.	_____	_____
4. He grew up and moved away.	_____	_____
5. He loved to ride his pony.	_____	_____
6. He learned new things from his friend.	_____	_____

REMEMBER Look for likenesses and differences.

Changes in the Forest

How are winter and summer alike? How are they different? In this lesson, you will read about animals and plants in the forest. You will learn to compare and contrast to find likenesses and differences.

▲ KEYS to Comparing and Contrasting

Alike or different?

LEARN When we tell how things are alike, we are comparing them. A bear and a cow are alike because they are both large animals.

A bear eats fish and berries, but a cow eats grass. When we tell how a bear and cow are different, we are contrasting them.

EXAMPLE Compare: A penny and a nickel are coins.
Contrast: A nickel is worth more than a penny.

DIRECTIONS Read each sentence. See if two things are being compared or contrasted. Print compare or contrast on the line.

1. A cup and glass are both used for drinking. _____

2. Summer and winter are seasons of the year. _____

3. Clockfaces have hands, but digital clocks do not. _____

4. Dads and grandpas are men. _____

5. Summer days are long, but winter days are short. _____

2 Practice Comparing and Contrasting

DIRECTIONS Read the following sentences. Think how the items are alike or how they are different. Use a word from the box to complete each sentence.

animals	holidays	cooks	green	gasoline	listen	croak
sells	keeps	bark	plants	land	fruit	eggs

1. A frog and a leaf are both _____, but a frog can

   _____ and a leaf cannot.

2. A banana is a _____, and so is an orange.

3. A dog and a lion are both _____, but a lion cannot

   _____ .

4. A petunia and a potato are both _____ .

5. Thanksgiving and Easter are _____, but _____
   are only decorated on Easter.

6. A stove _____ food, while a refrigerator _____ it
   cold.

7. A library loans books, but a bookstore _____ books.

8. A car and a truck both run on _____ .

9. Ducks and fish like water, but ducks can live on _____ .

10. Television and radio programs are alike because we can

    _____ to them.

DIRECTIONS Do changes in the weather cause changes in the lives of plants and animals? Read the story to see how plants and animals live in different seasons.

Changes in the seasons affect the lives of plants and animals in the forest. They know that spring is coming when the air gets warmer.

The snow melts and causes the earth to be wet and soft. Tiny roots push into the earth and plants grow. The sleeping animals wake up. Birds build nests and lay their eggs. Squirrels, rabbits, and bears find their mates and begin a new cycle of life.

The air gets hotter and the days grow longer. It is summer. Green plants are everywhere. They are food for all the new babies of the forest.

Plants and animals must work hard to stay alive. They need food and water. The animals who sleep all winter are getting fat. They are storing food for next winter. Other animals are storing food in hiding places to eat during the winter.

Then the air gets cooler, and the days get shorter. It is autumn or fall. Birds are flying south. Some animals are getting ready for their winter's nap. Leaves of many trees are turning red, yellow, and brown. The ground is getting cold and will soon be white with snow.

The ground gets colder and begins to freeze. Winter is here. The daylight hours are short. The trees shed their leaves. The green plants are gone now, but their seeds lay hidden underground.

The bears, woodchucks, snakes, and bats are sleeping. Squirrels, prairie dogs, and other animals discover that food is difficult to find now. They are glad they worked hard all summer, storing food in secret places. The plants and animals are waiting for the warm air of a new spring.

Read each question. Use the story you just read to complete the answers. Then think about your answers, and circle the correct word to tell whether you compared or contrasted.

1. How do birds and bears prepare for winter?

Birds _____ .

Bears _____

_____ .

compare   contrast

2. What must plants and animals have to stay alive?

Plants need _____

_____ .

Animals need _____

_____ .

compare   contrast

3. What do snakes and woodchucks do in winter?

Snakes _____ .

Woodchucks _____ .

compare   contrast

4. What are the days like in summer and in winter?

Summer days are _____ .

Winter days are _____ .

compare   contrast

Compare = Alike
Contrast = Different

Letters from Camp

In this lesson, you will read some letters about some strange-sounding things. Is that because words do not always mean just what they say?

 ## KEYS to Figures of Speech

Figures of speech give words special meanings.

LEARN Sometimes we use words in a way that gives them a special meaning. We call these words figures of speech.

EXAMPLE Tim's in a real jam.

Does this mean Tim is stuck in a jar of the sweet stuff you put on toast? No! It means he's in trouble.

DIRECTIONS Underline the figure of speech in each sentence.

1. Their team beat the socks off our team.

2. I know you don't believe me, but I'm not pulling your leg.

3. I passed the spelling test with flying colors.

4. She likes to tell stories, so take her words with a grain of salt.

Strawberry Jam

Practice With Figures of Speech

Read each sentence. Circle the letter of the group of words that tells the meaning of the underlined figure of speech.

1. I am so mad at my brother I will <u>give him a piece of my mind</u>.

    a. tell him just what I think
    b. give him part of my head

2. Mom was <u>tied up</u> in a meeting for two hours.

    a. bound with rope
    b. very busy

3. Grandpa was just <u>pulling our leg</u> about his pet dinosaur.

    a. tugging on our leg
    b. fooling us

4. This book <u>doesn't hold a candle to</u> the one I read last week.

    a. isn't as good as
    b. does not make a good candle holder

5. My sister <u>got wind of</u> our plans, and now she wants to go, too.

    a. heard about
    b. was hit by a strong wind

3 Read and Apply

DIRECTIONS Read Susan's letter to her brother. Then find each underlined figure of speech in the letter. Circle its real meaning.

Dear Jason,

My new friends and I are having fun here at camp. Some of us were **1.** feeling blue when we first got here. We missed our friends from home. Our counselor said she had a surprise to help us **2.** break the ice. We couldn't figure out what she meant. Then she **3.** let the cat out of the bag.

It was a scavenger hunt. That's when you have to find a bunch of things on a list. Well, this sent us on a **4.** wild goose chase. It was like **5.** looking for a needle in a haystack. We finally found everything and finished just **6.** under the wire.

We all think camp is fun now.

Love,
Susan

1. feeling glad   feeling sad

2. fall into the lake   get to know each other

3. told the secret   showed us her cat

4. goose hunt   long search

5. something hard to find   something very sharp

6. a little too late   in time

When Jason read over his answer to Susan, he thought it sounded dull. Help him make his letter more interesting by writing the number of the correct figure of speech on the line before each group of words in parentheses.

Dear Susan,

   I'm glad you're having fun at camp. This is what's been happening at home.
I gave a speech at the Fourth of July picnic yesterday. That's something that _____(doesn't happen very often). You would have been _____(very happy) if you could have heard me.

At first, though, I _____ (couldn't speak very clearly). I knew the words _____(perfectly), but I couldn't get them to come out right. I told myself to _____(stay calm). I took a big sip of water.

_____(Very quickly) my voice came back. Everything was fine. Everyone clapped when I finished.

                                   Love,
                                   Jason

1. happens once in a blue moon
2. by heart
3. had a frog in my throat
4. keep my head
5. pleased as Punch
6. before you could say Jack Robinson

REMEMBER Figures of speech make reading fun.

90 Figurative Language

The Pictures Tell the Story

Sometimes a picture can tell a story better than words. Sometimes the pictures help you understand the words better. In this lesson, you will learn to read charts with pictures on them. The charts will tell you more about people like you.

KEYS to Reading Charts

Charts show you what you want to know.

LEARN   Here are two ways to say the same thing.

Words:

It was 70 degrees on Monday,
65 degrees on Tuesday,
68 degrees on Wednesday,
69 degrees on Thursday,
72 degrees on Friday,
75 degrees on Saturday,
and 70 degrees on Sunday.

Chart:

	Mon	Tue	Wed	Thu	Fri	Sat	Sun
80°							
75°	70°	65°	67°	69°	72°	75°	70°

DIRECTIONS Use the words or the chart to answer the questions.

1. Which day was the warmest? _____

2. Was it warmer on Friday or Saturday? _____

3. Which days had the same temperature? _____

2 Practice Reading Charts

DIRECTIONS Study the chart. Answer the questions.

The students in Mrs. Clark's class kept a record of the books they read for two weeks. Then they made a chart to show what they found. Each picture stands for one book.

Books Read

Sports	📚📚📚📚📚📚📚
Animals	📚📚📚📚📚📚📚📚📚📚
People	📚📚📚📚📚
Places	📚📚📚📚

📚 = 1 Book

1. How many books about places did the class read? _____

2. What kind of books did the class read most often? _____

3. What kind of books did the class read least often? _____

4. How many sports books did the class read? _____

5. Did the class read more books about people or animals? _____

3   Read and Apply

DIRECTIONS Study the chart. Answer the questions.

The students in Mr. Parks' class saw the chart. They wanted to make one too. The two classes decided to make a chart together. They kept track of their books for two more weeks.

"This will be a really big chart," said Mr. Parks. "Can anyone think of a way to make the chart smaller and still show both classes?"

Delores raised her hand. "What if we made each picture stand for two books?" she said.

That's just what they did. They divided their chart into two parts. On the left side are books read by Mrs. Clark's class. On the right are books read by Mr. Parks' class.

	Mrs. Clark's Class	Mr. Parks' Class
Sports	▯▯▯	▯▯
Animals	▯▯▯▯▯	▯▯▯▯▯▮
People	▯▯▯▯	▯▯▯
Places	▯▯	▯▯▯▯

▯ = 2 Books

1. Which class read the most books? _____

2. Which class read the most animal books? _____

3. How many books about people did the two classes read together? _____

4. Which kind of book did the two classes together like least? _____

5. Which kind of book did the two classes together like most? _____

6. What do you think the half book stands for? _____

DIRECTIONS Since so many students liked books about animals, the students made a special chart. Study the chart. Answer the questions. Circle the letter of the best answer.

Books about Animals

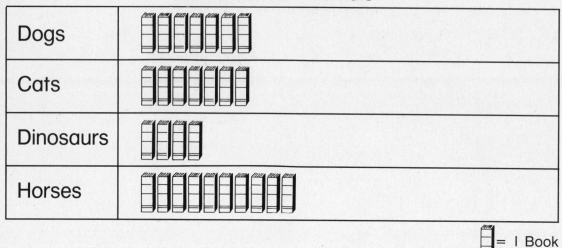

= 1 Book

1. How many books about horses did the class read?
   - **a.** 20
   - **b.** 10
   - **c.** 4

2. Which two kinds of animal books tied?
   - **a.** dinosaurs and dogs
   - **b.** cats and dogs
   - **c.** horses and dinosaurs

3. What animal did the students read about most?
   - **a.** horses
   - **b.** dogs
   - **c.** dinosaurs

4. How many books does each picture stand for?
   - **a.** 1
   - **b.** 2
   - **c.** 5

5. The smallest number of books was read about which animal?
   - **a.** horses
   - **b.** cats
   - **c.** dinosaurs

Read It Again

Sometimes you like a book so much you wish it would never end. In this lesson, you will use a title page to find more good books.

 ## KEYS to Using the Title Page

Title. Author. Date. Artist. Publisher.

LEARN You can find the title page near the beginning of every book. It gives special information.

DIRECTIONS Write the letter of the correct meaning on the line.

_____ **1.** author _____ **2.** title _____ **3.** illustrator _____ **4.** publisher

a. person who draws the pictures   **b.** company that made the book

c. person who wrote the book   **d.** name of the book

 ## 2 Practice Using the Title Page

DIRECTIONS Study the title page. Follow the directions.

1. Draw a box around the title.

2. Underline the author's name.

3. Circle the illustrator's name.

4. Draw a squiggly line under the name of the publisher.

> I Love Books
>
> by
>
> I. M. Arthur
>
> illustrated by
>
> Drew Moore
>
> Books, Incorporated
>
> New York

Read and Apply

DIRECTIONS Study the title pages. Answer the questions.

Modern Space Travel	Space Flights	A Trip to the Moon
by	by	by
R. Ocket	Jim Dandy	Will Write
illustrated by	illustrated by	illustrated by
Art Smith	Ann Artist	B. Good
Good Books, Inc.	Write On Co.	Story Press
Kalamazoo	New York	Chattanooga

1. Which book would you choose if . . .

    a. your favorite author were Jim Dandy? _____

    b. you enjoyed pictures drawn by Ann Artist? _____

2. Which publisher would you write to if you wanted _____
to contact Will Write?

3. In what city would you find the publisher of _____
Space Flights?

REMEMBER A title page can help you find more books you like.

Horse Sense

   If you wanted to get a horse or take riding lessons, what would you need to know? In this lesson, you will read about horses. You will learn about choosing the information you need.

KEYS to Choosing Important Information

Just read for the facts.

LEARN When you read for fun, you pay attention to all the words. When you read to find out, you might find more information than you need to know.

   Think about just what you want to find out. Always remember just why you are reading.

DIRECTIONS Read to find out what to feed a horse. Read the whole story. Underline the sentence that tells what you need to know.

   Debbie heard a whinny when she opened the barn door. She ran to Kelly, and gave her a hug. Then she grabbed the hay fork. Kelly was hungry. She needed fresh hay and a bucket of oats.

   Debbie picked up the wire brush. Kelly stood very still. She loved to be brushed.

   Debbie knew it was almost time to catch the school bus. She tossed some fresh straw into the stall. She gave Kelly fresh water and one more hug. Then she waved to Kelly and ran out the door.

DIRECTIONS Ken wants to take riding lessons. He found the ad below in the newspaper. Read the whole ad. Put a check on the line before each fact he needs to know.

Riding Lessons

Prairie View Stables

Over 100 stalls for boarding

Riding lessons Tuesday and Wednesday

10:00–11:00 a.m.

$12.00 per hour

We board cats and dogs, too.

For boarding information call 555-5556.

For riding lessons call 555-5555.

_____ 1. Riding lessons are at Prairie View Stables.

_____ 2. You can board cats and dogs at Prairie View Stables.

_____ 3. You can board your horse at Prairie View Stables.

_____ 4. Riding lessons are Tuesday and Wednesday from 10:00–11:00.

_____ 5. Riding lessons cost $12.00.

_____ 6. Call 555-5556 for boarding information.

_____ 7. Call 555-5555 to sign up for riding lessons.

DIRECTIONS Read to find out what the dawn horse looked like. Put a check on the line in front of each fact you need to know.

Millions of years ago, a small horse, the dawn horse, lived in North America. The dawn horse had a short neck. Its mane was made of a few stiff hairs. It had a small tail. Each front foot of the dawn horse had four toes. The back feet had only three toes. No one rode the tiny dawn horse. It was an ancestor of the horses we have today.

_____ 1. The dawn horse lived in North America.

_____ 2. The dawn horse had a short neck.

_____ 3. Its mane was made of a few stiff hairs.

_____ 4. It had a small tail.

_____ 5. Each front foot had four toes.

_____ 6. The back feet had only three toes.

_____ 7. No one rode the tiny dawn horse.

_____ 8. The dawn horse was an ancestor of the horses we have today.

DIRECTIONS Read to find out how horses of today look different fron the dawn horse. Fill in the blank to complete each fact. Draw a line through each sentence you don't need to use.

The horse of today looks far different from the dawn horse. It is much bigger. It has a long graceful neck. Its mane and tail are long and thick. It doesn't have any toes. It has strong hard hoofs.

Most horses today do not run wild. Horses today are large enough to be ridden. Before farmers had machines to help them with their work, they used horses.

1. Today's horses are much _____ than the dawn horse.

2. Its neck is much _____.

3. Its mane is _____ and _____.

4. The dawn horse had a _____ tail.

5. The feet of a dawn horse had _____.

6. The feet of today's horse have _____ _____.

REMEMBER Think about why you are reading.

Easy as ABC

A dictionary is a handy thing to have. It tells you how to say a word. It helps you understand what a word means. In this lesson, you will learn to find words quickly in a dictionary.

KEYS to Using a Dictionary

Guide Words. Entry Words. Alphabetical Order.

LEARN   All the words in a dictionary are in alphabetical order. If you know the alphabet, you can find any word. Alphabetical order is easy when all the words start with a different letter. If the words all start with the same letter, use the second letter to put them in order.

DIRECTIONS Write 1, 2, or 3 on the lines to show the correct alphabetical order of the words.

A. _____ bus

_____ better

_____ birdseed

B. _____ opera

_____ mountain

_____ onion

C. _____ heavy

_____ handle

_____ hiccup

Guide words are printed at the top of each page. They show you the first and last words on the page. They are in large type so you can see them more quickly. If the word you are looking for is between the guide words in the alphabet, it will be on that page.

Read the guide words in dark print. Read the list of words under each guide word. Cross out the words that would not be on that page.

1. snail/sniffle
snail
remember
speedboat
sneeze
snarl

2. Frankenstein/ freethrow
decay
potato
free
freckle
furniture

3. burglar/bus
burn
bus
addition
burro
legend

4. ladder/lance
lamb
ladybug
lake
iceberg
swarm

5. moneybags/ monopoly
meal
monkey
murmur
mongrel
none

6. condo/confetti
confetti
catcher
does
confess
bookcase

DIRECTIONS Each word with its definition is called an entry. An entry tells you four things. It shows you how to spell the word. It shows you how to say it. It tells you its part of speech. It tells you all the word's meanings. Sometimes the entry gives you a sentence to show you how to use the word.

How do you say it?   **What part of speech is it?**

hand·bag (hand′bag) *n.*   **1** a woman's pocketbook; purse.   **2** a small suitcase.

How do you spell it?   **What does it mean?**

DIRECTIONS Read the entries. Circle the correct answer for each question.

min·i·a·ture (min′ē ə chər *or* min′i chər) *n.*   **1** a very small copy or model [a *miniature* of the Liberty Bell].   **2** a very small painting, especially a portrait. *adj.* that is a miniature [a *miniature* railroad].

min·now (min′ō) *n.*   **1** a very small fish of the carp family, found in fresh water and used as bait.   **2** any very small fish.

1. Which word means a <u>very small fish</u>?   miniature   minnow

2. Which word can be pronounced in two different ways?   miniature   minnow

3. Which word is divided into two parts, or syllables?   miniature   minnow

4. Which word can be two different parts of speech?   miniature   minnow

Hera/hermit

He-ra (hir'ə) the Greek goddess of marriage, who was the wife of Zeus. The Romans called her *Juno.*

herb (urb *or* hurb) *n.* any plant whose stems and leaves wither after the growing season each year; especially, any such plant used as a medicine, seasoning. etc. [Mint and sage are *herbs.*]

her-bi-cide (hur'bə sīd *or* urb'bə sīd) *n.* any poison used to kill plants, especially weeds.

her-biv-o-rous (hə biv'ər əs) *adj.* feeding mainly on grass or other plants [Cows and deer are *herbivorous.*]

Her-e-ford (hur'fərd *or* her'ə fərd) *n.* a breed of beef cattle with a white face and a red body. *See the picture.*

her-mit (hur'mit) *n.* a person who lives alone, away from others, often for religious reasons.

Hereford

1. What are the guide words on this page? _____

_____

2. Which word means <u>plant</u>? _____

3. Which word means <u>something you can use to kill plants</u>? _____

4. How many words are nouns (n.)? _____

5. How many meanings does each word on this page have? _____

6. Which word has just one part, or syllable? _____

7. How many entries are on this page? _____

REMEMBER A dictionary tells what a word means.

Using the Encyclopedia

When you want to find something out in a hurry, the encyclopedia can help you. The encyclopedia is a little bit like a huge dictionary. You can find information about almost any topic.

In this lesson, you will practice finding information in an encyclopedia.

 ## KEYS to Using the Encyclopedia

Encyclopedias tell you what you want to know.

LEARN An encyclopedia is something like a dictionary. The words are in alphabetical order. The encyclopedia is much larger, though. It gives more information about each entry.

Most encyclopedias have more than one book. Each book is called a volume. The letters on the spine tell what letter the words inside begin with.

DIRECTIONS Look at the set of encyclopedias on the shelf. Find the number of the volume that contains each entry. Write it on the line.

A-C	D-F	G-I	J-K	L-M	N-P	Q-R	S	T-V	W-Z
VOL.1	VOL.2	VOL.3	VOL.4	VOL.5	VOL.6	VOL.7	VOL.8	VOL.9	VOL.10

_____ 1. monkeys

_____ 2. zebras

_____ 3. automobiles

_____ 4. soccer

_____ 5. Africa

_____ 6. quartz

_____ 7. denim

_____ 8. pianos

_____ 9. volcanoes

2 Practice Using the Encyclopedia

DIRECTIONS The hardest part of using the encyclopedia is deciding which word to look up. Practice finding the key word in the questions. Write the word you would look up on the line.

1. Who invented kites? _____

2. What are the names of the provinces in Canada? _____

3. Did George Washington really chop down his father's cherry tree? _____

4. How big do lions get? _____

5. What country put up the first space satellite? _____

6. How do you play checkers? _____

7. What is the largest city in England? _____

8. What does a Cocker Spaniel look like? _____

9. Are there different breeds of cats? _____

10. Who were the Pilgrims? _____

11. How many rings does Saturn have? _____

12. What did dinosaurs eat? _____

3 Read and Apply

DIRECTIONS What do you do with the information you find in the encyclopedia? Usually you tell someone else or write a report. When you write a report, you need to make the information shorter. You need to put it in your own words.

Read the information from the encyclopedia. See how Dana changed the information into her own words. Fill in the blanks to complete her story. Use synonyms to replace the words in the encyclopedia.

Hummingbirds are the smallest birds in the world. They are called hummingbirds because their wings make a humming sound. The smallest hummingbird is the size of a bumblebee. The largest hummingbird lives in South America. It can grow to be 9 inches (23 centimeters) long.

Hummingbirds can fly up, down, backward, or forward. They can fly very fast. These colorful birds can have patches of green, purple, red, and orange. They

have long thin beaks. Their beaks are especially made for sucking nectar from flowers.

Hummingbirds are very _____. They get
their name from the _____ from their
                          1
wings. Some hummingbirds are the size of
                    2
a _____. Some are much _____.
      3   4
Hummingbirds fly in every _____.
                                          5
They fly _____. Their bills are long
                  6
and _____. Their feathers have pretty
          7
_____. _____
      8

Read the encyclopedia entry about the mountain lion. Use the lines to write about the mountain lion in your own words. Don't try to write everything. Just write what interests you.

Mountain lions are members of the cat family. Before the settlers came, mountain lions lived all over the United States and in the southern part of Canada. Now the few that are left live in the far West. Some live in Louisiana and Florida.

Mountain lions can be gray, red, or yellow, with white fur on their stomachs. Some are pure black. They may grow to be 7 to 8 feet long, including their tail.

Some people do not like mountain lions. They say they kill cattle and pets. They are afraid mountain lions will attack them. Scientists say people must be careful not to kill all the mountain lions. They usually will not attack people. They eat sick animals, who might give their disease to other animals.

_____

_____

_____

_____

_____

_____

_____

_____

_____

_____

_____

REMEMBER Find it fast in the encyclopedia.

Sorting It Out

When you go to the store, it's easy to find what you want. The same kinds of things are all in the same place. In this lesson, you will learn to sort out your ideas. You will see what it would be like to work in a store.

 ## KEYS to Categorizing

Categories are groups of things that are alike.

LEARN When you sort things into categories, you put together ideas that have something in common.

DIRECTIONS Put the words into the best category.

picnics	dimes	arithmetic	sisters
swimming	sleds	cardinal	snowmen
science	robin	pennies	uncles

1. Winter Fun: _____ _____

2. Summer Fun: _____ _____

3. Birds: _____ _____

4. School Subjects: _____ _____

5. Relatives: _____ _____

6. Coins: _____ _____

DIRECTIONS Play the **In and Out Game.** The clues tell you what is in the category and what is not. Write the name of the category on the line.

1. _____

Susie is out.
Bobby is in.
Angela is out.
Diego is in.
Mary Jo is out.
Martin is in.

2. _____

Elephants are out.
Goldfish are in.
Tigers are out.
Kittens are in.
Bears are out.
Dogs are in.

3. _____

Apples are in.
Records are out.
Hamburgers are in.
Money is out.
Carrots are in.
Cars are out.

4. _____

Dolls are in.
Schoolbooks are out.
Baseballs are in.
Lawnmowers are out.
Games are in.
Knives are out.

Read and Apply

DIRECTIONS Help Mildred the grocer put her store back together. Write the names of the products on the right labels.

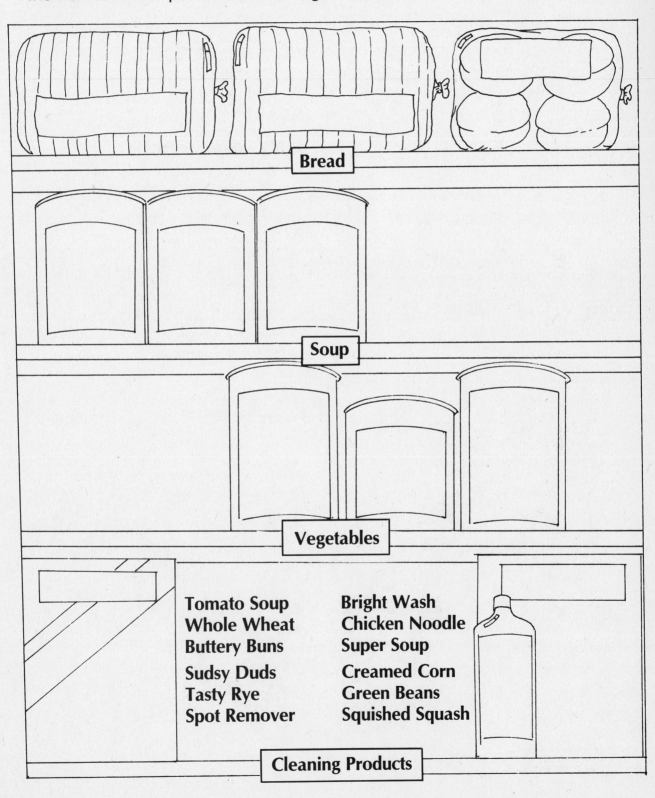

Bread

Soup

Vegetables

Tomato Soup   Bright Wash
Whole Wheat   Chicken Noodle
Buttery Buns   Super Soup

Sudsy Duds   Creamed Corn
Tasty Rye   Green Beans
Spot Remover   Squished Squash

Cleaning Products

DIRECTIONS Read the list of categories. Think of four things that fit in each category. Write them on the lines.

1. Holidays

_____

_____

_____

_____

4. TV Shows I Like

_____

_____

_____

_____

2. My Classmates

_____

_____

_____

_____

5. My Favorite Foods

_____

_____

_____

_____

3. Books I Have Read

_____

_____

_____

_____

6. Games I Like to Play

_____

_____

_____

_____

REMEMBER Categories are groups.

But the monkeys only shook
their fingers back at him and said,
"Tsk! Tsk! Tsk!"

The peddler was angry. He
shook his finger at the monkeys
and shouted, **"You monkeys you!
Give me back my caps!"**

The peddler became more angry. He shook his fist at the monkeys and shouted, "**You monkeys you! Give me back my caps!**"

The peddler just stood there. Then he looked up into the tree. On every branch there was a monkey and on every monkey there was a cap—
a yellow cap,
a red cap,
a blue cap,
or a green cap.
The peddler looked at the monkeys. The monkeys looked at the peddler.

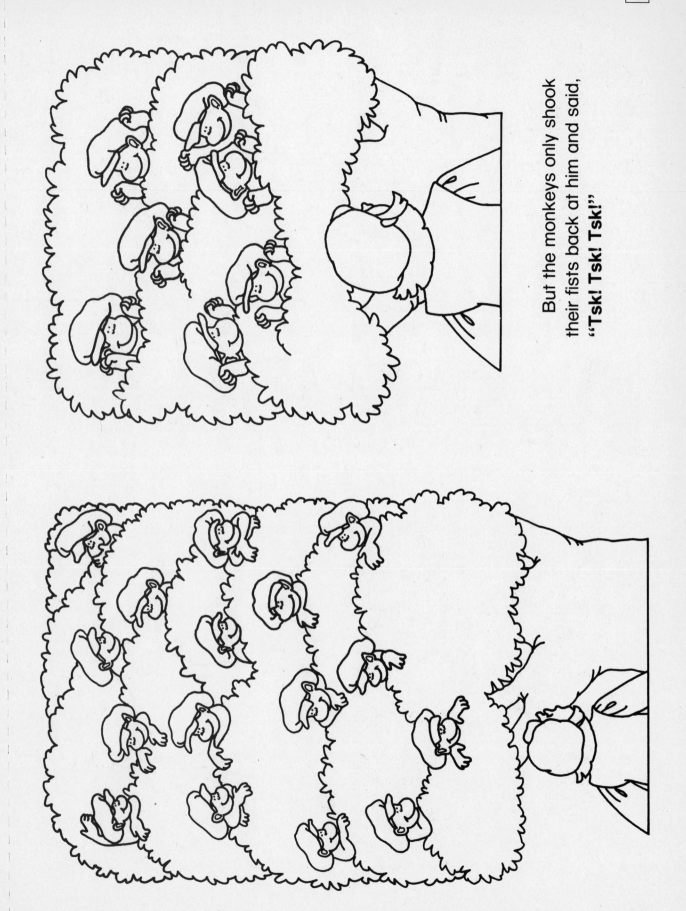

But the monkeys only shook
their fists back at him and said,
"Tsk! Tsk! Tsk!"

15

10

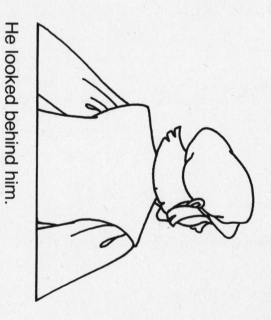

He looked behind him.

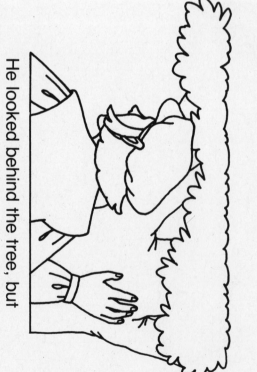

He looked behind the tree, but the caps were nowhere to be seen.

The peddler became even more angry. He stamped his feet at the monkeys and shouted, **"You monkeys you! Give me back my caps!"**

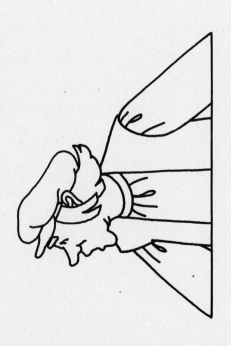

He looked to the right of him.

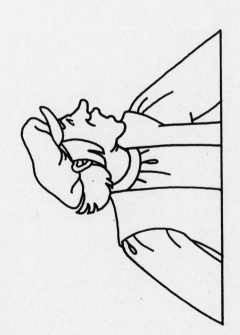

He looked to the left of him.

At last he woke up. The first thing he did was to reach up and make sure that his caps were all safe. But all he could feel was his own brown cap. All the other caps had gone!

But the monkeys only stamped their feet back at him and said, **"Tsk! Tsk! Tsk!"** The monkeys did not understand why the peddler was shouting at them. But they did know that they were having lots of fun copying him. And they liked the caps—
yellow caps,
red caps,
blue caps,
and green caps

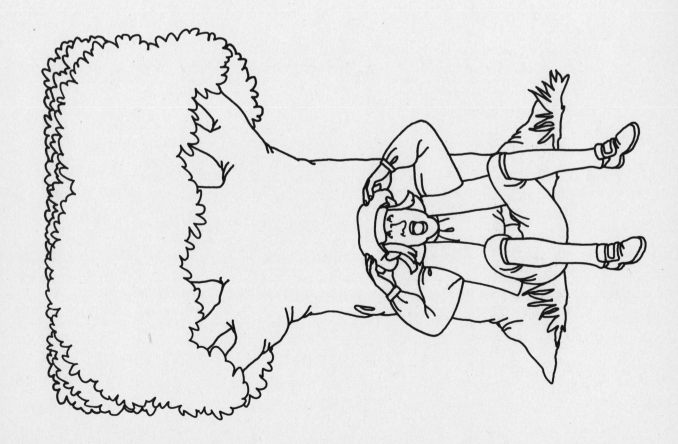

He walked and walked until he
came to a great big tree. He sat
down underneath the tree and
reached up to make sure that his
caps were straight.
Then he went to sleep. He slept
for a long time.

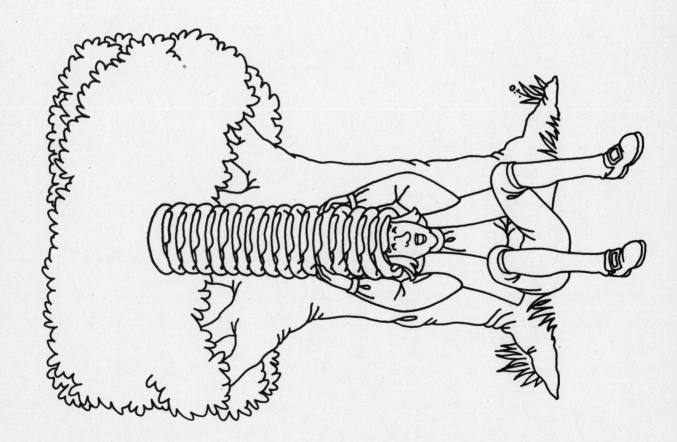

Now the peddler was really angry. He took off his own brown cap, threw it onto the ground and shouted, **"You monkeys you! Give me back my caps!"**

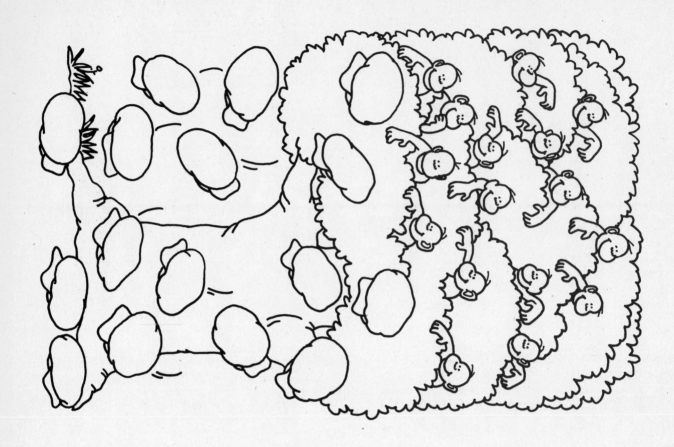

After the peddler had walked up
and down the streets all morning
he felt hot and tired. He thought
that he would have a rest.

And with that, all the monkeys
pulled off their caps,
the yellow caps,
the red caps,
the blue caps,
and the green caps,
and threw them to the ground.

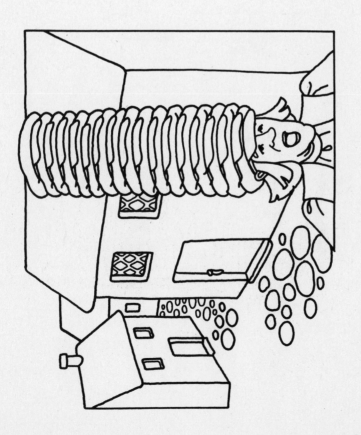

Off he went, up and down the
streets, calling out loudly, "Caps
for sale! Caps for sale! Only 50
cents a cap!"

Now on this morning nobody
bought any caps—not even one.

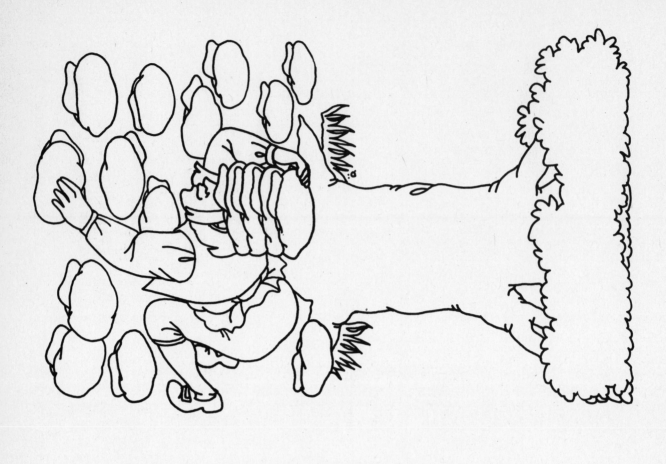

Once upon a time there lived a peddler who sold caps.

He carried the caps on top of his head. First he put on his own old brown cap. On top of his own brown cap, he put four yellow caps. On top of the yellow caps, he put four red caps. On top of the red caps, he put four blue caps. And on top of the blue caps, he put four green caps.

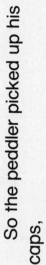

So the peddler picked up his caps,

first his own brown cap,
then the four yellow caps,
then the four red caps,
then the four blue caps,
and then the four green caps.

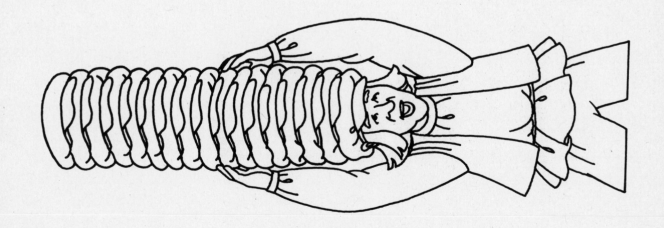

Then he walked up and down the streets calling out loudly, "Caps for sale! Caps for sale! Only 50 cents a cap."

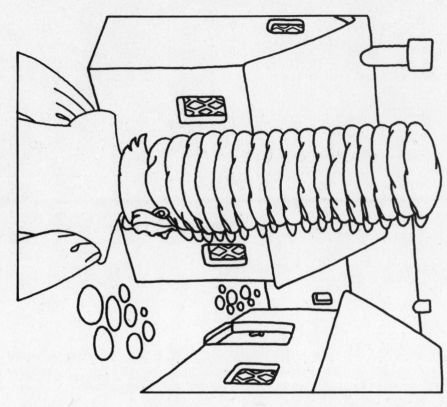

The Peddler's Tale
Retold by
Mary O'Toole